About the portrait of Frederic Loomis on page 8:
"The charcoal drawings of doctors prominent in Peralta's early days ...
were done by artist Peter Van Vaulkenberg. The first drawing was of
Dr. Loomis and the second of Dr. John Sherrick, his associate — the
price $50 apiece. This totaled the $100 for the care of the artist's
wife at the birth of their baby. George Wood, then superintendent
of Peralta, and a neighbor of the artist, arranged the exchange of ser-
vices, and Dr. Loomis liked to tell that he had traded a baby for the
picture. Later, other doctors who admired the artist's work had their
pictures drawn."

—from *The Peraltan*, a publication of Peralta Hospital (now Summit
Medical Center), Oakland, Calif., November 1972.

Printed in the United States of America
First printed August 2000
Hardscratch Press, Walnut Creek, California

Library of Congress Catalog Card Number: 00-091208
ISBN: 0-9625429-9-7

0 9 8 7 6 5 4 3 2 1

Miner, Preacher, Doctor, Teacher

This book is dedicated to my sisters, Hilary
and Julie, and cousins Fritz and Judy,
in memory of our grandparents,
Edith and Frederic Loomis.

Ketchikan waterfront, c. 1904.

Peter Van Valkenburg
January 1932

Frederic W. Loomis

Introduction

I never really knew my grandfather, Dr. Frederic Loomis. I remember at age four sitting on his lap and seeing, for the first time, what a magnifying glass could do to a young boy's thumb — wow, it got big! I knew that he was a famous doctor and had written some books.

Fifty years after that enlarged thumb, I inherited from my mother a box of his writings in typescript form, a major portion of them autobiographical and concentrating on his years as a young man in Alaska. Now these tales have become his final book.

My grandfather loved to write and tell stories. He wrote about Michigan, his home state, and about Oregon, where he attended rodeos in later life, as well as about his early years in Alaska. He wrote stories with moral lessons, stories about the practice of medicine, stories about the curmudgeons, rapscallions and other characters he had encountered in his life. (These stories often held moral lessons, too.) In 1938, the year he retired from medical practice, he published a best-selling book, *Consultation Room*. A sequel, *The Bond Between Us,* was published in 1944. He wrote for *Reader's Digest, Coronet, This Week* and other periodicals.

Frederic Morris Loomis was born April 12, 1877, in Ann Arbor, Michigan, the first child of Mary E. McMahon Loomis, from County Clare, Ireland, and Frank C. Loomis, a harness-maker. He had one sister, Marie. His childhood escapades included wiring his neighborhood for covert amateur telegraph transmissions, playing tricks on the family housekeeper, and performing first aid on local cats in preparation for a medical career. He entered the University of Michigan in 1894 as a pre-med student.

Halfway through, after his first year as a full-fledged medical student, family finances dictated that he take a year off from his studies. The sinking of the battleship *Maine* in 1898 and the ensuing Spanish-American War took him to the southeastern United

States and brought him in close contact with Theodore Roosevelt, although by a fluke he never saw action. Soon after the war, he went to Southeast Alaska to look after his father's mining interests in Dolomi, across Clarence Strait from Ketchikan.

The record does not show exactly when he first went to Alaska, but it was probably about 1900. His own writings, which pick up after his arrival at Ketchikan, reveal that initially he was more an administrator for the Alpha Mining Company than a miner. He returned briefly to Michigan in 1901 or 1902. Back soon in Dolomi, he became a hardrock miner with a man named H.J. Garness, who according to the stories had been his frontier mentor during that first year in Alaska. Together they worked the Fortune mine. The colorful tales in this book relate the rest of his Alaskan experience better than any summary here could.

Mining, primarily for gold but also silver and copper, began in the Dolomi area of Prince of Wales Island in 1898. Gold had been discovered there by a Native boy named Paul Johnson, who found gold-bearing quartz on the north shore of Paul Lake as he waited with a canoe while his father hunted deer. In 1902, Dolomi consisted of a store, a small wharf, a sawmill and a post office. Its population reached a high of 50 in 1904, the year the post office was transferred to Ketchikan, and then began to decline. Eventually there were at least 19 mining claims in the Dolomi area. The most developed were the Valparaiso and the Golden Fleece. Trams were built to these mines at Paul Lake and James Lake to haul out rock and ore. By 1920, most mining had been abandoned on that part of the island, and today it is difficult even to find the old sites in the dense undergrowth that rapidly reclaimed them.

Ketchikan was the hub for mining activity in the area when my grandfather arrived. Originally a Tlingit Indian fishing settlement, it was incorporated on August 25, 1900, and is now Alaska's fourth-largest city. A year-in-review issue of the Ketchikan *Mining Journal* newspaper, January 1907, reports that "Frederick M. Loomis, the superintendent of the Alpha company and who is so prominently connected with other properties at Dolomi, is a young man of energy and ability. ..." Under the heading "St. John's Mission," the paper has kind words for his future wife, "Miss Prichard, the present teacher of the school," whose work "is a living testimonial of her conservation and fitness. ... Cleanliness, order, diligence and loyalty suitably describe the school under her care ..."

There are some gaps in the timelines offered in several of my grandfather's tales. We do know that he married my grandmother, Edith Prichard, on January 1, 1907. She moved to Dolomi from Ketchikan in March 1907, and they lived in a small house on Dolomi Bay. Later that year they began planning for a return to Michigan and medical school. From mid-1907 until September 1908, my grandmother taught again in the Episcopal missionary school in Ketchikan, the position that had drawn her to Alaska. My grandfather worked for the newspaper, served for a time as lay-man-in-charge at St. John's Episcopal church, and did other work to supplement their income.

Back in Michigan, they rented a large house and took in students as boarders. My grandfather, who had first entered college at 17, received his M.D. in 1912 at the age of 36. He interned in obstetrics and gynecology at the University of Michigan until 1916. Then, when he was 40, he and my grandmother and their two daughters (my mother and her older sister) migrated west to Oakland, California.

He quickly established the first specialized practice for women in Oakland. He was the first to use a portable nitrous-oxide gas machine for anesthesia, a machine he had brought from Ann Arbor. But he was best known for his ability to make his patients feel cared for and comfortable in his presence.

As this formerly rough-and-ready frontiersman wrote in *Consultation Room*: "The birth of her first baby is the most thrilling physical and emotional adventure in a woman's life. Whether the memory is to be sweet or bitter depends not only on the technical skill of her doctor but upon his ability, as well, to satisfy her in-

11

stinctive longing for security and to give her the comfortable feeling that she is the only person in the world at that moment who deeply concerns him; that his one thought is to bring her back safely."

In 1938 he retired from practice, but only after having delivered more than 3,000 babies. He spent subsequent years traveling and writing. He died in 1949, with these stories of his time in Alaska unpublished.

I knew less about my grandmother, Edith Prichard Loomis, until I naively decided to publish these Alaska tales. Six months pregnant with their third child, she died in 1917 during the worldwide influenza epidemic. My mother, now deceased, was three and a half when her mother died; she remembered very little. So I had only my grandfather's stories and one photograph to know my grandmother by.

But after my mother died, in 1996, my sisters and I found several photo albums from Alaska among her keepsakes. Many of the photographs they contained had been taken by my grandmother, and some are reproduced here. The missionary archives of the Episcopal Church yielded letters she had written. And her delightful and detailed account of the 1916 trip by car from Michigan to California turned up [Chapter XV], along with her diary; several Alaska passages from the diary also appear here. This unknown woman, whose portraits show that she strongly resembles my mother and sisters, began to take on more substantial form for me.

Edith Amelia Prichard was born in Russell, Kentucky, in 1877 or 1878, one of a family of five girls and two boys. Early in her life her father, William W. Prichard, died. The two brothers had left to seek their fortunes, never to be heard from again.

Her mother, Olive W. Prichard, moved the five girls to Boston, "where," she often declared in later life, "the center of education was." There she opened a boarding house near Radcliffe College. The daughters were instructed that they should not sew — that eyes should be saved for reading. Edith graduated from Boston

Latin Academy (then Girls Latin). In 1903, at the age of 26, intelligent, educated, attractive and as yet unmarried, she signed on to teach for five years in a missionary school in Alaska. Her sister Ruth was married to the Rt. Rev. Thomas Jenkins, who at that time was the mission minister at St. John's Church in Ketchikan.

From my grandfather's tales it is apparent not only that my grandmother was instrumental in convincing him to return to school but that she provided "the gentler touch" that complemented him in Dolomi, Ketchikan, Ann Arbor, and finally Oakland.

My grandfather could spin a good yarn. In these stories, written perhaps 30 years after his time in Alaska, he is guilty of a little hyperbole, a few inconsistencies, and some omissions of date and time. But these minor literary aberrations do not distract from the dual theme of the tales: his unabashed joy in the adventure of life on Clarence Strait in the pioneer days of the early 1900s, and his decision to apply the same hard work and dedication to becoming a noted doctor and raconteur.

One cannot study tales of turn-of-the-century Alaska and the missionary presence there without becoming aware of some differences between the Native and white cultures. It needs to be noted that the dilution of Native culture began long before any churches were asked by the U.S. government to bring educators to Alaska in the 1850s.

The enormous profits reaped by the Russians and then by the Spanish, English and Americans in the sea otter trade of the 18th and early 19th centuries had a devastating impact on Native life. Then, in the mid-19th century, came mining, timber harvesting, and finally the rush for gold. The white attitude exemplified in the phrase "primitive faith," for instance, represents not a church attitude but an attitude of the times, with a strong historical tie to phrases like "Manifest Destiny." I am not a student of Alaskan history and am not in a position to reflect in any depth on the cultural evolution of Alaska Natives. But even the negative aspects of the missionary presence in Alaska seem benign in comparison with what the Spanish Franciscans effected in California from 1770 to 1830. That may not excuse any paternalistic attitudes on the part of my grandfather's generation, but it does, I believe, put them in perspective.

If any of these stories offend, my sincere apologies. We have attempted in editing to balance between those times and our own.

Many have supported the scholarly aspects of this book. They are named, with gratitude, in the Acknowledgements. Any errors or omissions are my own. I would also like to thank my wife, Bonnie, who married into a much larger family than she anticipated, for patience, encouragement, and comfort. My sisters, Hilary and Julie, and cousins Fritz and Judy for digging into dusty boxes and graciously supporting this project. And Jackie Pels of Hardscratch Press, whose editing, prodding, wisdom and technical resources made this book a reality; thanks to designer David Johnson it is a handsome reality.

A final note, for Alaskans present, past and future.

On New Year's Eve in Ann Arbor, Michigan, 1911, my grandmother wrote in her journal:

> *12/31/11—Quiet day—Fred busy with lecture & I feeding and caring for F.M. [daughter]. Cold very bad. Seemed like an Alaskan day—so quiet.*

I hope that readers of my grandfather's tales will relish being transported to those rough-and-tumble times at Dolomi. I also hope that you can envision the quiet Alaskan days.

Lee Sims
El Granada, California

I
My First Voyage

I successfully completed my first operation at the age of eight, and I made my first voyage aboard a ship of my own design and construction when I had just turned 11. Many people would say, I imagine, that this was a trifle young to show such a strong inclination toward both medicine and travel. But at this moment I am a practicing doctor, and in the course of my lifetime I have seen the world. Which proves, I guess, the old saying that you can do anything if you have a mind to do it.

At the particular time when I was spread-eagling the family cat atop my mother's clean white ironing board, and poking away at pussy's paw, the path to medicine looked very simple: merely a succession of ironing boards, and small victims, until I should someday succeed to an operating board of my own. I did not know then that the way to the operating table would point via the detour of the wild forests and icy waters of Alaska. But as things turned out, I became a sort of pioneer before I became a doctor, and this is the story of one tenderfoot's experience on the Last Frontier, when the hoarse cry of "Gold!" was echoed in a million brassbound throats, and desperate men risked life and health to wrest the precious ore from the mountains and streams where it was hiding.

But I'm getting ahead of myself. If this is going to be an adventure story, I had better begin with my first adventure.

"But, Mother! I can too build a boat! A good boat, plenty good enough to float down the river to Big Lake. Why, it's only 50 miles or so . . ."

I was terribly aware that my voice had taken on a certain pleading note that my mother disliked.

But it was so hard to speak calmly when one was forced to trot around her in our kitchen, as she moved back and forth from breadboard to oven, from oven to breadboard.

"I don't think so, Fred. You're much too young."

"But Tom's going, too. We're going to build it together . . . and he's almost 12 . . . three months older'n me."

"I," said my mother wearily.

"Older'n I, I mean, and besides, what could happen to him and I . . .?"

"Which eye?" asked Mother.

"Him and me, and anyway, it's perfectly safe . . . and . . ."

"Let's not talk about it anymore. You've never built a boat, you've never even seen one built, and it can't be done anyway by two such small boys. Better forget it, Fred."

"But if we could build it," I persisted, "and if it was a good boat, and Daddy said yes?"

"Well," Mother conceded in a confident tone, "if it was a very good boat, and your father and I approved . . ."

"Thank you, Mother!" I shouted, and tore out of the kitchen, down the back steps, across the dusty back yard, through the gate with a bang, and so into the alley to the Lair, the architectural wonder that was Tom's and my precedent for shipbuilding. Cracker-box in shape, motley in color, ramshackle in degree of repair, the Lair was a lopsided construction of stolen fence boards, flattened tin cans and packing boxes. Through the ingenious use of ropes and props and slings we had even managed to suspend a second floor, which sagged perilously under the slightest tread. The upper room was furnished with an empty orange crate and a broken-down rattan chair, our pride, the strands of which offered emergency cigarette makings that we pulled off to smoke, with burning eyes and blistered tongues, when we ran short of corn silk and dried clover.

At the door of the Lair I slid to a stop and gave the secret "Kee-wee" whistle for safe entry. The Lair boasted a metal welcome mat that was wired to the door handle and formed a circuit with the electric light current running to Tom's house (somewhat reduced by a homemade rheostat). We were thus assured that no unwelcome visitor would long lay hand upon our means of entry.

Tom's answering "Kee-wee" gave me leave to dash through the door. I restored the electric current to the handle and joyfully announced: "I can go! If it's a good boat. Now, where are we going to get lumber?"

Over the next few days, mysteriously, materials began to amass themselves. Cellars received an unexpected cleaning, garage doors vanished off their hinges in the night, broken fences evaporated, and odd planks and boards became nonexistent.

Tom's family's barn was the setting for our endeavor, and for four weeks such a racket of pounding issued from that impromptu shipyard as to make the neighbors hold their ears in wonder and dismay. Our building plans were simple. We desired utility in preference to grace or beauty, and utility, after a fashion, was what we got. The mind of a boy is not tortured by complicated ideas of beauty—the classical and functional square was good enough for us, and square our ship was indeed. Had several of our most vital planks not possessed a slight warp of their own, I'm afraid the boat would have had no curve at all.

With perfect seriousness, we named her "The Swan." We fervently hoped she would take after her namesake, and float. My father's comment when he was permitted a preview was that The Swan was more like Scandinavian Lena, whose step made the dishes rattle in our kitchen: square as to sides, blunt at both ends, and tapering nowhere. As Lena's father had put it: "She ain't so pretty for handsome—but she ban sure for strong!"

Finally The Swan was ready, painted by strange chance the color of a neighbor's house that was undergoing renovation at the time. With barely suppressed excitement we invited our parents to a ceremony in the barn, where we peeled off the old canvas with which we had her covered. The Swan stood up stately, if landbound, on wooden horses amidst the straw flooring of the barn.

My father's face was a contortion of amazement and amusement and parental pride.

"Isn't she beautiful, Dad? Well, isn't she?"

My father seldom spluttered, and I knew he was in the grip of great emotion. "Well, son. That's—that's a boat!"

My mother was more skeptical. She viewed the caulkings and the ballast with alarm. "But, son—will it float? That's what I want to know. What makes you think it will float?"

Tom and I looked at each other in disgust. Women and boats—the two just didn't mix! I thrust my hands deep in my pockets and rocked a little on my heels. The fact that I nearly lost balance did not alter the nautical nature of my stance.

"Avast, madam!" I cried. "Don't insult our hulk here! She's seaworthy, all right!" My father smiled at my mother. "We've lost a son, my dear. But maybe this jolly young tar will visit us now and then when he gets home from his travels!"

I looked at him with disbelief. Could it be that he was telling me I might go—I really might go down the river in our boat? I was almost disappointed—I had been braced for a siege of pleading and wheedling. But my parents kept their word. The Swan was seaworthy, we knew we had built her well, and now we were ready to go!

What a flurry of packing and preparation! Tom and I spent the better part of a week amassing maps and charts, lanterns, tarred ropes, canvas, bedclothes, and a peculiar array of clothes which we thought to look "nautical."

My father entered into the spirit of adventure and rented a wagon to haul the boat over to the river. There, in a quiet eddy, we launched her.

"Hadn't we better christen her, Fred?" Tom asked. "All boats are christened."

"What with?"

"Here, I brought along a bottle of catsup."

"Then you christen, and I'll say words over her."

The only trouble was the catsup bottle was so thick it would not break. Tom whanged away until we had dented the wood so deeply we were afraid The Swan might leak. We compromised by shaking the contents of the catsup bottle over some sandwiches we had brought along.

On the day we were to hoist anchor and put out to sea (on the placid river), about 10 of our buddies turned out to see us off. With what envy they stared at us, with what immeasurable pride we strutted the postage stamp deck of The Swan! At the word, my father, who had kindly consented to act as longshoreman, cast us off from the moorings, and as the current caught our craft in its embrace we sailed majestically out, out, out ... for 10 feet. A gentle scrape brought us up short. We were aground!

Horrified, we peered over the gunwales. The raucous jeers of the watchers on the dock blistered our ears. Yes, we were aground, all right—stove up on a little sandbar barely submerged under the waterline. And there we sat, helpless, until my father took mercy on us, rolled up his trousers, and waded in to re-launch us.

The five days and nights of our voyage were filled with mystery and high adventure. Every whisper of the gentle stream, every flop of a fish, every night cry of a strange bird spelled out delicious excitement for our 11-year-old souls. Eagerly we awaited what lay beyond the next bend of the river. We hardened ourselves against the onslaughts of mosquitoes, flies and sunburn, and took pride in our stoic courage; the wiggle of a water snake, the terrifying hoot of a lonely owl on the shore thrilled us; the exquisite scent of our own fresh-caught fish, burning in a blackened skillet, tantalized our nostrils. Golden days—wonderful days—never to be forgotten! The lures of all the travels of the world were captured in that 50-mile float down a lazy river in the state of Michigan.

Tom and I talked very little throughout the voyage. The first day we played at being sailormen. We "avasted" and "aye-aye'd" each other half to death; and then the reality of our boat trip became more enticing than play-acting, and we settled down to what we were, boys experiencing their first great adventure.

The morning of the fourth day I shall never forget. We rose for breakfast in the silver light of the early dawn, unknotted our leg muscles, unkinked our stiffened backs—and discovered that our stupendous appetites had caused a dreadful shortage of food.

"What are we going to do?" I cried, for the absence of food was unthinkable.

"Live off the land," answered Tom bravely. "Like the pioneers did."

An exciting thought—but once we had slipped over the side of The Swan and paddled to shore, the prospect of pitting our cunning against the forest primeval became less appealing. Try as we might, we could not scare up a bird, a rabbit or a squirrel. And the fish had gone into hiding.

The thought of starving to death, owing to 24 hours without nourishment, was monstrous. At that moment a gun report echoed in the trees.

"Somebody's hunting! Maybe they'll give us some of their game!"

Another report.

"That's coming from the shore."

"Maybe somebody's trying to steal our boat!"

The thought was enough to take precedence over hunger. We sped back through the thicket toward the boat mooring. As we burst out of the brush bordering the shallow strip of sand where we had beached The Swan, we saw that we had company. Moored in a tiny cove not more than 50 yards away was a houseboat, a ramshackle, broken-down affair patched together with odd strips and pieces of lumber, crowned by a small stack that sent forth wisps of gray smoke. Something else issued from the houseboat, too, and wafted its way over to the little sand strip where we stood watching. The tantalizing odor of breakfast!

"Let's go over, Fred," whispered Tom. "Maybe they'd offer us some."

Just then came another gunshot, so loud as to nearly shatter our eardrums, and out of the door of the cabin burst a straggle-haired woman. Behind her was a man, clad only in ragged pants, armed with the biggest, longest shotgun I had ever seen. The wispy woman screamed and fled out of sight around the cabin, the man in pursuit. In a moment she reappeared at the other end of the cabin, still screaming. As she made a dash for the door, the man stopped, dropped on one knee, leveled his gun at her—and fired. The shot whizzed by her shoulder. She screamed and raced again around the cabin with the man tearing after her.

Tom and I stood horrified. We expected at any minute to see the gun-crazed fellow bring her down with a well-aimed shot. And we would be the witnesses to a murder!

"Tom! What'll we do?"

"You can do what you want to, but I'm getting out of here!"

Tom slipped silently into the water, and I followed him. We submerged and paddled underwater out to The Swan. Dripping and gasping for breath, I hoisted myself up to the deck as Tom was feverishly loosening the mooring rope. Just as he got it undone and prepared to cast off, we heard another blood-chilling shriek. We flattened on the deck of The Swan and watched. The gunman fired, missed, she screamed, and they leaped around the deck in a frenzy. Suddenly the man stopped, threw back his head like a dog, and sniffed in our direction.

Then, without warning, he brought up his gun, looked down the barrel, and fired a volley straight at us! I yelled and dropped on my face. Tom, who was still holding the mooring rope in his hands, felt a jerk. The rope flew out of his hands, shot in two!

Shells kicked up vicious little spurts in the water around us. Buckshot thudded into the wooden sides of The Swan with a dull thwack that chilled our marrow. But the river took mercy.

A gentle eddy of the current coiled itself around The Swan and tucked it out into the slipstream. While we huddled like little mummies on the deck, The Swan picked up speed in the main current and began to drift farther and farther away from the houseboat.

The riverman fired twice more, and then we heard nothing. By the time we gathered enough courage to lift ourselves off the bottom of the boat, we had rounded a curve and the houseboat was out of sight.

Then I heard a howl go up from Tom. A bullet had nicked his finger and he was bleeding vigorously. This gave me a chance to tend him with all the care of a surgeon general. Hoping for some such opportunity, I had stocked The Swan with medical equipment, so I spent a good half-hour treating his wound.

By common consent, neither Tom nor I spoke of the incident after we returned home. The rest of that day was filled with re-hashing the event, building up our roles in the drama, and conjecturing about the mystery of the gun-crazed riverman. But a sixth sense warned us that if we ever expected to take another voyage on The Swan our parents must never hear of the incident. And they never did.

II
The Would-be M.D. Becomes a P-v-t.

The other day I queried our paper delivery boy as to what he was spending his money for, and he replied that he was saving to take flying lessons. I reflected that when I was growing up, the air was thought of only as a medium through which telegraph wires could be strung. Amateur telegraphy was the rage of the age.

I too delivered papers, carrying them to 140 subscribers in homes strung out over a seven-mile distance. It wasn't much fun delivering the Grand Rapids Herald to customers in the middle of a Michigan winter, I can tell you. My pals and I spent every penny earned—my "take" was the enormous sum of one dollar and 25 cents a week—for telegraph instruments. We balanced ourselves on the ridged poles of our neighbors' barns to fasten our insulators, and finally succeeded in stringing out a line that was several miles long. I fastened an elaborate switchboard of spring brass and made a portable sending set that I could take to bed with me.

It was wonderful to snuggle in bed, heaped high with patch-work quilts and "comforters," and talk by wire to my friends all over the city, our sounders screwed down to a mere click to escape our parents' notice. Of course, the inevitable occurred: My father learned my call letters, RH, secretly taught himself the code, and laboriously would tick out, "C-o-m-e—h-o-m-e" at times when otherwise I would have been beyond his reach.

I can still read the Morse code if it isn't sent too fast, and can send with reasonable speed and accuracy. I have ticked out "no" or "yes" more than once with a pencil or table knife to one who could understand when difficult questions were being decided.

In the several years that I was engaged in the pursuit of telegraphy, little Arthur, the son of my father's business partner, Aaron Vandenberg, followed me around and begged me to teach him the Morse code. My buddies and I would run away from him and even climb 70-foot telephone poles to escape. Sitting regally astride the top crossbars, making believe that we were linemen, we would smile down at Arthur while we nonchalantly munched our lunches. By Irish luck we were never caught there, either by the real linemen or by our parents.

Little Arthur now owns the paper that I once carried, but our country knows him best as the distinguished senior senator from Michigan who has made so brilliant a record in Washington. Perhaps I should have relented and taught him the Morse code, though he seems to have done very well without it.

A few months after my 17th birthdate, I entered the university, taking it for granted as I had since I could remember that in six years I would have earned the degree of Bachelor of Arts and Doctor of Medicine. It is easy to take things for granted at 17! I plunged into my fifth year of Latin, and my third year of Greek, with university mathematics and French, and waited impatiently to begin Medicine. In the meantime I found I could not play baseball quite well enough to make the varsity team but did become an editor of the university daily and in time became the sporting editor, so I could travel with the team and report the home games as well.

All this was ended when in my third year I began the study of medicine.

There was no daylight left when our laboratories closed, and very little had appeared when we began classes in the morning. My days were filled with "ologies"—bacteriology, osteology, histology; with general and qualitative and physiology chemistry—each more wonderful and tougher than the other.

Dr. Novy, world famous, became *spirillum rubrum* to us, as, coiling his long legs around the speaker's stand, his red hair shining, he tried to teach us that a germ was a vegetable organism and not an animal. Dr. Vincent C. Vaughan, dean of the department and recipient of every honor known to American medicine, was loved as "Piggie" Vaughan. He opened our eyes to the mysteries of the amino acids and other end products of digestion and their final elimination from the body. His course, physiological chemistry, was appropriately abbreviated to "P Chem."

We all felt sorry for the poor devils who were studying futile and relatively useless things like the Fine Arts or Law, future teachers and lawyers who would never see the amazing intricacy of the inside of a human body and—much worse—in their benighted ignorance would never even want to. What they thought of us, and said to us, at dinner after a long hot afternoon in the dissecting room pawing over the brachial plexus or the perineum of a citizen long since deceased, requires very little elaboration. Scrub as we might, they knew when we were coming and never detained us when we left. I think modern methods of preparation of the subjects for dissection have materially lessened the odor of sanctity which surrounded us then. We rather liked it—it identified us as "medics."

I learned how to work. No one lasts long in a medical school who doesn't. I wish some effective way could be found to teach youngsters how to study before they come so handicapped by being allowed to play at it—to study with the radio going full blast, for example. I know—at least I have heard it often enough— that they insist that they can study geometry or Latin even better with a jazz band going; and at the end of the month the poor marks are practically always the fault of a "dumb teacher," not of the band!

The year was over almost before I knew it. I could hardly wait for the next one to begin. But on my return home at the end of the term, I found that things had not gone well with my family financially, and that my slender allowance had become a heavy burden. I saw at once that I could be useful in many ways if I stayed out of school for a year.

Eager as I had been to go ahead with medicine, I set to it gladly. The mind at 20 is so easily adjustable. There was the chance to do something for my father and mother who had done so much for me, and the prospect of a year at home with them, broken by trips on the road as a salesman, made it easy to change my plans. I knew that it was only for a year, anyway. Or I thought I knew.

My first road trip began on my 21st birthday, April 12, 1898. The country was ablaze with the sinking of the *Maine*, and at my first stop I found a telegram ordering me to return for duty with the National Guard company I had joined as a rear rank private.

There followed the excitement of recruiting, of drilling the rookies in the armory and in the streets at night. The flag-waving and the cheers, and finally the departure for the state encampment at Island Lake. Then sudden apprehension when we heard that scores of recruits were being thrown out because of varicocele, a highly selective and blameless male complaint very prevalent at the time, probably because nearly all of us rode bicycles constantly. The orderly rows of tents containing less orderly rows of prospective soldiers lying flat on their backs with ice bags tightly applied to highly localized areas, under expert advice, to minimize the danger of rejection. The great day of the examination itself. And finally the orders to leave at once for Tampa, Florida, for service in Cuba.

None of us had seen the South, the great fields covered with the rich dark green of tobacco leaves alternated with seas of waving bolls, dazzling in the sun. Every little house along the way exploded in a cascade of shy waves and shining eyes and wide smiles whenever the train slowed down; and at the stations pretty girls gathered in curiosity to see the Yankee soldiers, sometimes trading kisses for brass buttons. The shortage of buttons became acute, and we saved what we had left by fastening them on with heavy safety pins that did not show.

In Tampa, of the many regiments camped around us, our nearest neighbors and best friends were the famous 69th New York, a thousand or more wild Irishmen from the Bowery. I think we all crawled thousands of miles on our bellies over Florida's scrub palmetto, training for the Cuban campaign. It was almost midsummer, and our heavy Springfield rifles were so hot in the sun that the barrels were almost blistering to touch.

Ybor City is or was just outside Tampa proper. In it was concentrated everything beyond the limits of everything proper—the beer halls, the scum of the white, black and brown women of every clime, the thieves and robbers and pimps, the cribs and dumps and dark alleys—all arranged for soldiers' pay days and all working nicely at top speed.

Details of 30 or 40 men were sent from designated companies for provost guard duty each day and night, not to conduct a Sunday School but to put a reasonable limit to the business of raising hell. If any local police were on duty, I don't remember them, and I don't believe they would have lasted long. It was all right to get drunk, but if a soldier fell on his face and stayed there obstructing traffic, he woke with his headache in the provost guard house, which was usually comfortably filled by morning, and whatever money he had was still in his pockets. It was within the bounds of righteousness for a dozen to crowd together into a pleasure-lady's boudoir and to entertain her with a song, but when they were moved to drop her dresser out her window or toss her in a blanket without benefit of clothing, it took only a shriek or two to bring help.

Like the Italian *carabinieri* we traveled in pairs, and usually only a word was enough to stop a disturbance. The Regulars looked down with great contempt on the Volunteers, and their kindest name for us was "lousy tin soldiers." But as a rule the soldier's respect for the uniform penetrated even his alcoholic daze, possibly because he had been taught discipline and perhaps because sidearms and a loaded rifle meant something to him.

There were exceptions. At the door of a beer hall, a soldier, one of the regulars, became too obnoxious and hostile, and coming up behind him I suddenly pinioned his arms from the rear. As his arms were jerked backward his left hand fell against the projecting end of my own bayonet hanging from my side. With a scream of rage he jerked his arm free from mine, my bayonet in his hand, and whirled on me, stabbing viciously at the middle of my stomach as he turned. Just at the split second that the bayonet touched my blouse, my best friend, Warren Morrill, now a distinguished doctor, whirled too, and smashed him in the head with the butt of his rifle, knocking him into the gutter—a complete casualty for the evening. That one was fairly close.

Just before we were to sail for Cuba, an officer from Colonel Theodore Roosevelt's Rough Riders appeared one day in our company street and to my astonishment offered me a place in his troop—in fact two places, not because I could ride especially well, but because they had two vacancies to fill and this chap had happened to hear that our company had many university men. He in turn happened to belong to my college fraternity—a new measure of eligibility of which possibly Colonel Roosevelt was not aware!

By that time I had become a sergeant. I knew I would have to take a reduction in rank and suspected that I might be left, as a new man, in charge of a lot of horses when the unmounted Rough Riders sailed for Cuba. I thought the smart thing to do was to stay with my own outfit to ensure getting over. I gave up the offered place to a lad in a neighboring company who actually did go over with them, went up San Juan Hill, and began then the career that has made him one of the significant men of the nation: Frank Knox of Chicago, later made Secretary of the Navy by President Franklin Roosevelt.

And in retribution for my being too smart, our ship broke down just before we were to sail. San Juan was taken, and we went back to the months of futile drilling and finally were sent home and discharged when the Spanish war was over.

This has always seemed one of the major mistakes of my life, and I have never ceased to regret it.

A little later when Colonel Roosevelt was traveling out West, they wanted someone who knew him or had been around him as sort of a bodyguard, and I was chosen for that. I was quite close to him, after all.

One day we were in a large city where they had a tremendous parade because he was the famous Colonel Roosevelt who had gone up San Juan Hill. They gave me a big horse to ride in the very front of the procession—in fact, right in front of Theodore Roosevelt's carriage. It had formerly been a circus horse, but I didn't know that. I got on it and led the procession, with Colonel Roosevelt directly behind me. But the horse wanted to dance to the music. There was a fine band, and he wanted to dance, and dance backwards at that. We started up the street and the band would start playing and the horse would turn around and around, and go backwards almost looking into Colonel Roosevelt's carriage. I talked to the horse (with words more suitable for the congregation at Ybor), but he paid no heed. Meanwhile, Colonel Roosevelt was responding to the applause of the crowds by taking off his hat and waving with both arms. Every time the horse turned around, he laughed a booming "Har, har, har." He had more fun than anyone else in the parade, though he wore out his arm taking off his hat so many times, and wore out his jaws laughing so hard at me.

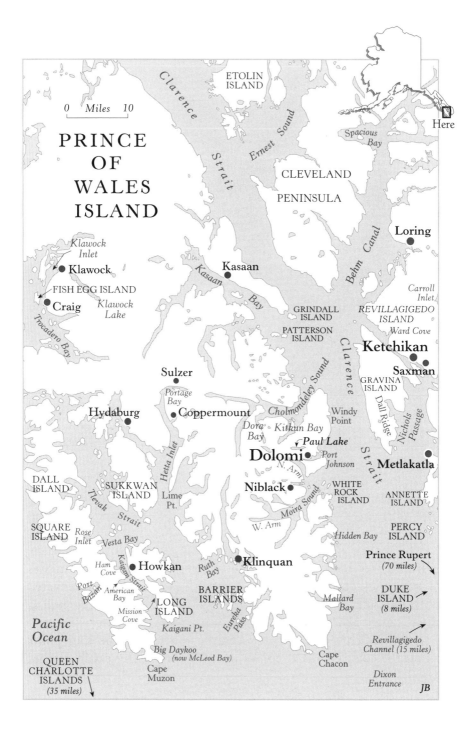

PRINCE
OF
WALES
ISLAND

0 *Miles* 10

Clarence

ETOLIN
ISLAND

Ernest Sound

Strait

*Spacious
Bay*

CLEVELAND

PENINSULA

Here

*Klawock
Inlet*

● Klawock

Kasaan Bay

Kasaan

Behm Canal

● Loring

*Carroll
Inlet*

FISH EGG ISLAND

● Craig

*Klawock
Lake*

Trocadero Bay

GRINDALL
ISLAND

PATTERSON
ISLAND

REVILLAGIGEDO
ISLAND

Ward Cove

Ketchikan ●

● Sulzer

*Portage
Bay*

● Coppermount

Cholmondeley Sound

Clarence

Saxman ● ●

GRAVINA
ISLAND

Hydaburg ●

*Dora
Bay*

Kitkun Bay

Windy
Point

Dall Ridge

Nichols Passage

Hetta Inlet

Dolomi ●

Paul Lake
●

*Port
Johnson*

Strait

Metlakatla ●

N. Arm

Niblack ●

WHITE
ROCK
ISLAND

ANNETTE
ISLAND

DALL
ISLAND

SUKKWAN
ISLAND

Lime
Pt.

Moira Sound

Tlevak Strait

SQUARE
ISLAND

*Rose
Inlet*

Vesta Bay

W. Arm

Hidden Bay

PERCY
ISLAND

Prince Rupert
(70 miles)

*Ham
Cove*

● Howkan

Kaigani Strait

*Ruth
Bay*

● Klinquan

DUKE
ISLAND
(8 miles)

*Port
Bazan*

*American
Bay*

LONG
ISLAND

BARRIER
ISLANDS

*Mallard
Bay*

*Revillagigedo
Channel (15 miles)*

*Mission
Cove*

Kaigani Pt.

Eureka Pass

*Pacific
Ocean*

Big Daykoo
(now McLeod Bay)

Cape
Muzon

Cape
Chacon

*Dixon
Entrance*

QUEEN
CHARLOTTE
ISLANDS
(35 miles)

JB

III

A Cheechako Lives Up to His Name

The first few weeks while I was settling into my Alaskan home, I studied in my spare time a map of Prince of Wales Island, and the shoreline, so that I might familiarize myself with all the names and locales mentioned in the old-timers' conversations. I learned that Southeast Alaska is indented by countless inlets or fjords reaching deep into the shoreline. These deep inlets and bays make it possible to reach hundreds of square miles which otherwise would be almost impossible to explore, and the sheltering, protective shores offer safe anchorage from the howling northern gales that rage up and down the open sea.

The southeasterly islands are heavily timbered with spruce, hemlock and cedar, and the ground is overgrown with thick masses of wild huckleberry and "devil's club," a cactus-like plant covered with thousands of sharp spines that bury themselves in the flesh at the slightest touch—an invention of the devil, I'm sure!

All through the winter, practically every day, the rain pours along the coast, while it snows in the interior. The brush catches

Above: The harbor at Dolomi.

and holds the water, and anyone trying to break trail through the brush is soaked to the skin in a matter of seconds. The only relief from such uncomfortable travel is to follow the countless game trails formed by generations of deer and bear, although a game trail does not guarantee that you will ever arrive at your intended destination.

It seemed to me at first that my entire day was spent in drying out and changing clothes. And of course, in the wet air, laundered clothes took longer to dry. Several times I remained inside, huddled in blankets, without a dry stitch to my name. Later I fitted into the routine of the Southeast Alaska frontiersman: Get up and dress, prepare breakfast, eat, go outside to do the chores, return, change clothes, hike to the mine and remove all outer garments and dry them out; hike home in the evening, change clothes. I think the smell of wet clothes, strung up before the blazing stove in my shack, will remain with me for the rest of my life.

The first week I was on the island I proved just what a tenderfoot—or cheechako, as Alaskans say—I was. My nearest neighbor, a Norwegian named Garness, had given me a prize, a pair of chewed, handsewn high-topped moccasins for winter wear. In spite of their apparent thinness, moccasins keep the feet dry and warm, because the skins are water-repellent to a large degree. On the day I chose to wear them "to break them in"—as if you needed to break in moccasins—I had stumbled through a puddle of water and soaked my feet. I returned home and put the moccasins under the hissing stove to dry out. A little later Garness came over for supper.

He sniffed suspiciously. "What you figuring to feed me tonight, Fred—stewed skunk?"

I breathed deeply. There was a burning odor vaguely akin to that of an animal. "I—I don't know what that smell is, Garness. But it's not supper."

He eyed me keenly. "You fool cheechako—you don't have those moccasins cooking, do you?"

Lord, the moccasins! I dragged them out—they were charred at the edges and absolutely stiff. The raging heat of the stove had dried out all the natural oils of the leather, and they were like potato chips—crackling, ready to fall apart. Garness looked daggers at me.

"If you don't have any better sense, you can get your damn-fool feet wet! You aren't getting any more presents from me!"

He kept his word. The next pair of moccasins I bought for myself.

A stray dog that had frightened me soon after my arrival, when I mistook it for a bear in the brush, became a great favorite and companion. In spite of the fact that there was much of interest to do, see and learn, the long Alaskan nights were lonely. Garness was indeed my nearest neighbor, but he lived over a mile away. After a hard day's work in the forests or the mines, few men feel like conversation. So usually, I found myself alone with Blackie, as I called him. He was not a particularly intelligent dog, but he had a sweet nature, and I came to love him.

After I had had him a few weeks, I mentioned to Garness that Blackie would disappear into a forest for hours at a time and then reappear winded and exhausted. This seemed strange, and Garness noted him sharply.

"Fred, that dog has been up to some devilment."

"Devilment? What can a dog get into in the woods?"

Garness leaned on his pick and ejected a stream of tobacco from between his jagged front teeth. "I'll tell you what—the pooch has been chasing young deer."

I was unimpressed. What dog didn't chase other animals?

"Yessir," Garness went on, "he's a deer chaser, and we're going to catch him at it."

The next time Blackie set off at a lope into the deep thickets, we followed him. Soon we heard an excited baying, and then the snap of twigs, high yelps and barks—and finally silence. A minute later we found him, sniffing eagerly at the carcass of a tiny baby deer.

"I thought so," said Garness grimly. "Look—he hasn't worried it any, just run it to death. Well, Fred, your pooch has got to go."

"Why? Is it a crime for dogs to chase wild animals?"

"In this country it is. Those deer are our food—sometimes all the meat we get, and we can't have young deer destroyed. Nope—you've got to get rid of Blackie."

There was no argument for that. I took the dog down to the boat landing and left him with Tim, the caretaker, to give to Captain Dodd the next time he came in from Ketchikan with the mail and supplies. I wrote a note asking Dodd to deliver the dog to a friend of mine in Ketchikan, so I would have Blackie when I went down there. I hoped that some day I could train him out of his deer-chasing habits.

Tim saw that I was broken up about saying goodbye to my dog. He offered me a half-grown black and white cat for company. I figured that a cat certainly wouldn't be a deer-chaser, so I carried her home and set her down on Blackie's old deer skin. Garness and I named her Beauty.

She became quite a household pet, of course, and I taught her to answer my whistle, like a dog. Beauty developed the habit of snuggling down underneath the wood stove to keep warm, and after a while the hair was completely singed off her back from the heat of the fire. A few weeks later when she too disappeared into the woods, an old prospector, Jeff Westlake, remembered about my cat with the singed back, and put her up for me until I could get to his cabin to fetch her home again.

Garness was my greatest friend and advisor. I don't know what I would have done the first few months without him. He taught me how to hunt wild game, for I had only shot cottontails and birds during my boyhood in Michigan. He taught me how to break trail, and camp in the wilderness; he explained the principles of placer and quartz mining, for my company had a stake in both; he guided me in the purchase of clothes and materials and supplies; he introduced me to the white people in the settlement and helped me make friends with the Indians.

Of course, it takes a long time to learn the customs and requirements in a new country. Just as winter was settling in I made a terrible and ignorant mistake that rightly incurred the wrath of Garness.

A bitter rain had fallen all day, and toward nightfall the temperature began to drop. By the time I had hiked back the five miles from the mine to my cabin I was soaking wet, tired and freezing cold. Nearing my cabin, which stood forlorn and bleak in the little clearing, the thought hit me that I had completely run out of stacked firewood. Before I could build a fire and make my supper, or even dry out, I would have to chop a couple of logs. How tiresome! Shivering, teeth knocking together, I looked for my ax, which was always left leaning against the outside of my cabin. It was gone!

This was strange. It was an unwritten law in the North not to steal a man's ax, since often his very life depended on being able to chop firewood quickly. What could have happened to mine? I searched quickly, getting colder by the minute. Finally I realized that my wet clothes were beginning to freeze on my body. This was dangerous, and I knew that I must do something, quickly. The nearest cabin was Garness'. I set out at a jog trot for it, and as I ran, my garments grew stiffer and stiffer and more heavy. My limbs were burning with that peculiar sensation that comes before they, too, freeze. My joints ached, my breath came in gasps, and my lungs felt as if someone had put a sword through them.

Finally, out of the night, a faint yellow glow loomed up ahead, a warm, welcoming signal. Garness' cabin! Half-dead I stumbled to the door and beat on it.

"Garness! Open up!"

Why was he so slow in coming? Then I heard a ponderous tread, the sound of a hand on the latch, and the door swung open. Garness stood, looking at me.

"What do you want, Loomis?" His voice was stern.

"For heaven's sake, let me in! I'm freezing to death, man!" I pushed him aside and almost fell through the door. The warm, steamy air curled itself around me, and the overpowering heat from the stove greeted me almost tenderly. For a second I stood drinking warmth in to my stiffened body.

Then I saw it! My ax—leaning against Garness' bunk!

There was somebody in the bunk, too—an old man, swathed in blankets, his pinched, straggle-bearded face peering out at me with hard eyes.

I spun around to Garness. "What the devil are you doing with my ax?"

"I took it."

"Took it? My ax? Do you know you nearly killed me! I about froze to death getting over here." I could have beat his face in with my bare hands.

"That so?" Garness' Norwegian features were as stolid as granite.

"Yes, that's so! And I want an explanation!"

Garness walked very close and glared down at me from his six-foot-two-inch height. "Listen, chee-chako," he grated, spitting out the words like bullets. "And don't ever forget what I'm telling you. In this country a man never leaves his shack without leaving at least one stack of wood to start a fire. That's friendly, see . . . that's neighborly . . . that's thoughtful! You never can tell when some poor devil like this one here —"and he jerked his head toward the shivering wreck in the bunk, "will stumble into your shack, half-frozen, needing a fire quick! And you, cheechako—you didn't leave him any firewood!"

He turned aside as if my crime was more than any man could bear, and spat. With unerring aim he hit the stove broadside and the moisture sizzled for a second on the blazing iron. I stood rebuked, silent, struck by his words and my folly in breaking this unwritten code of the North.

"I—I'm sorry."

"Sorry! So would Ben here be sorry if he froze to death!" The silence in the cabin was thick. Then Garness jerked his head toward the ax.

"There's your ax, Loomis. Take it, and get out!"

I looked at him, thinking he had suddenly lost his mind. Take it and get out? Half frozen, stiff with ice, my blood congealing in my veins—and he was sentencing me to sure death in the outdoors? Get out? A mile to my own cabin, and then, faint with cold, to chop wood? Garness was pronouncing my death warrant! But at the same time I realized that with awful justice he was meting out to me the fate that I in my carelessness had offered to the old prospector.

There was nothing more to say. If I made it back, and could keep moving long enough to chop up some wood, I would live. If I didn't make it, well, I just wouldn't. It was Northern justice. I reached for my ax and slowly moved for the door. With my hand on the latch I hesitated, half expecting Garness to relent. No word came. There was justice but no mercy in Alaska. I opened the door and stepped into the icy air.

I will never know how I made it back to my cabin. If the trip to Garness' cabin was hell, it was agony twice over going back. The brief warmth inside the shack had thawed my clothes just a little, and with the first impact of the air they froze all over again. The stiffened cloth rubbed and scraped my flesh like knives, the wind flayed me.

When finally I stumbled in sight of my cabin, my strength was gone, my bones were brittle points of agony. I could scarcely grip the ax in my frozen fingers, let alone swing it. With a last surge of effort I fell through the door into my shack and lay panting on the packed-dirt floor. Then—through ice-rimmed eyes I saw the stove, neatly packed with chopped firewood, waiting for a match to be put to it. I mustered strength—for that one match.

And while the heat curled around me—welcome, life-restoring warmth—I knew that Garness' justice was tempered with mercy after all. He had sent me back on a road of death so that I would never forget; he had laid the fire so that I might live—and always remember!

IV

Buck Fever, and Hard Luck Lucky

Hunting in Alaska is more than a sport. It is a necessity, if one expects to eat fresh meat at all. I soon found this out. The only meat available to us was dried beef, and canned meats that were tasteless and totally unsatisfying. When a man works hard in the mines, or hews trees all day long, his mouth waters for fresh, juicy meat! The only solution was to go out and shoot it.

During my first few weeks, Garness kept me in meat, since we were eating together, but after about a month had passed he suggested one day that I had better be laying in the winter stock.

"Winter stock? What do you mean?"

"Listen, you're going to get plenty meat-hungry about midwinter. Better lay in a couple of deer and some bear meat—and some salt fish."

This made good sense, so the next day I took off from my accounting work, shouldered my carbine, stuffed a sandwich into my pocket along with some shells, and started for the hills. Near our mining camp, far back in the island interior, was a large lake, a couple of miles long. An old miner, De Young, who had lived on

"Trying to hang on to my precious trophy, I completely lost my balance and tumbled into one of those infernal prickly bushes called devil's club ..."

the island for half his lifetime and consequently looked like part of the foliage, rowed me in his skiff up to the head of the lake, where absolutely virgin forest lay all around us for miles.

I'd been told that this stretch of land held the best hunting on the island, and I felt sure that if I spent the day roaming the thickly forested hills I would flush out a deer. I had never shot a deer, true, but I had accompanied Garness on two deer hunts. I knew that if you stalked near their regular water trails, sooner or later you would sight one—and if you were downwind, the animal wouldn't smell the human scent and be frightened away.

It had rained very hard, and the trees and brush were heavy with moisture. The ground was wet, too, and this was to my advantage, for the twigs were so sodden they didn't snap under my tread. I found a small hillock, overlooking a break in the underbrush, which I was sure was a game crossing. I cocked my gun and settled down to wait.

An hour went by. I was getting stiff, and bored. Suddenly an almost electric thrill passed through me. The air seemed charged with a new vitality, and I was positive, with what I would now call a hunter's sixth sense, that my quarry was nearby. I eased myself to a standing position and peered over the little rise of ground.

My quarry stood alerted by the slight movement, a true king of the forest, an eight-antlered buck, poised, listening. One more sound, and he would have been gone with lightning swiftness, but on the other hand, one squeeze of the trigger, and I would have my deer.

I was frozen, rigid, unable to pull that trigger! Hunters say that the first time any gamester sights his first deer he is frozen, just as I was, with a sort of wonder and awe. This sort of momentary paralysis is called "buck fever," and I was suffering from a severe attack of "buck fever." Try as I might, I could not fire the shot that would bring down my game, although I had him, dead center in my gunsight.

While I stood there, with my muscles turned to water, the proud animal slowly turned his head and gazed straight in my direction. I knew that his short-sighted eyes could not see me, half hidden in the foliage, and I knew the wind was blowing my scent away from him, but it was almost as if he knew that I was there, waiting for the strength to kill him.

Then in a rush the "fever" passed, and I pulled the trigger. The carbine report sounded like thunder in my ears, but the bullet found its mark. For a split second the animal still stood, proud, calm. Then it dropped in its tracks. I had shot my first deer!

Dead game must be bled right away, so while the reverberation of the gunshot was still quivering away in the silent mountain air, I hurried over to the buck. I reached for the head to expose the throat, so that I could quickly cut it and let out the blood, but just then the deer moved, rolled its saucer-like brown eyes upward and rattled in its throat. This almost unnerved me. I felt like a murderer, looking down into the living face of my victim. But I knew that the poor thing must be in agony from the shot. I drew out my hasp knife and put a speedy end to the buck's suffering. I let the blood, and then prepared to hoist the deer, Indian-fashion, to my back to carry it the two or three miles to the head of the lake.

I succeeded in hoisting the animal crosswise on my back, legs hanging down over my shoulders, and I staggered a few hundred yards with it. But it was too heavy. I knew I couldn't make it. What to do? I decided to cut a protective sledge of thick branches, place the deer carcass on this, and drag it. But the thought came to me that the head, with those proud antlers, would make a magnificent trophy mounted in my shack. Besides, they were the antlers from my first deer.

So I removed the head from the body to protect it, placed the carcass on the branch sled, and attempted once more to make my way back to the lake, this time carrying the head. Shortly I came to a steep slope, where I rolled the body of the animal to the bottom and then started to follow, with the head. Halfway down I slipped in the mud. With my arms flailing wildly, but trying to hang on to my precious trophy, I completely lost my balance and tumbled into one of those infernal prickly bushes called devil's club. My trousers ripped in the process, and my legs were full of thorns.

At that moment, I realized that in my excitement over tracking the deer I had neglected to blaze trail with my hand hatchet on the trees. I was lost! Thoroughly and completely lost!

"If Garness could see me now," I thought with grim amusement. Here I was, the conquering hero, with a buck's head slung over my shoulder, and I didn't have the faintest notion of how to find my way home.

Then I remembered that De Young had remarked that all the mountain streams in these parts fed into the lake. Obviously, the thing to do was to follow the downward course of a stream.

I started along the bank, still dragging my deer and shouldering the head, but I kept slipping into the water. It was deep and swift and strong, so it seemed reasonable, since I was wet already, to wade down the stream bed and float the body of the deer.

By this time the incessant rain had started again. I was utterly miserable. My trousers hung in raggedy strips and I was sopping and desperately hungry, since in my headlong tumble I had lost my sandwich as well as my dignity. Lightning zigzagged across a sullen sky, and hoarse rolls of thunder punctuated each flash. Wading in the midst of a stream of water was not the safest place to be.

With no warning, I stepped into a sinkhole in the stream bed and went down. Wildly I clutched for support as I sank, and let go carbine, deer head, and the leg I was holding of the carcass. I strangled, kicked violently, and in a moment, my feet found a firm footing again. I set about retrieving the deer, the deer head and the rifle.

I looked at my gun. It was soaked and would not shoot again

until it had been dried and cleaned. I took comfort in the thought that now, at least, I wouldn't be shooting myself in the leg.

The stream began to gather force and I realized that I must be nearing the head of the lake. What a relief! But I was so exhausted that I knew I couldn't carry or even drag the deer carcass one more foot. I also couldn't abandon it in the forest. With the fall of night, a dozen hungry and ravening wolves would be at the meat, and morning would reveal only whitened bones.

If only I could put it up somewhere, out of their reach. In a small clearing I saw two saplings, standing about six feet apart. Now to hoist that deer of mine up, out of any wolves' reach, and sling it between those two young trees. Thanks to Garness I had a rope with me, neatly coiled and buckled to my belt. As I unfastened it, I thought of his warning:

"Fred, don't ever go off by yourself without three things—a gun, a knife and a rope!"

I bound the legs of the deer tightly and hoisted the carcass up between the saplings. I lashed the rope securely and left it there, looking like a strange wash that had been hung out on a line to dry. But my pride wouldn't let me leave the deer head. Tired though I was, I was determined to carry it home.

Without further mishap I followed the stream on down to the head of the lake. Half an hour's hike around the curved shore line, and I was tapping on De Young's cabin door, after stashing the deer head out of sight.

He burst into laughter when he caught sight of me.

"Cheechako!" he roared. "If you ain't the sorriest looking hunter I ever saw!" Tears of mirth rolled down his cheeks as he cackled. "Too bad, fella, better luck next time! Maybe you'll catch a deer instead of a drowning!"

"I got a deer."

"G'wan with you and your tales! Deer! I don't see no deer!"

I smiled, for I had waited for this. I edged outside the cabin and hoisted the deer head in my arms.

"Look here, De Young. What do you call this—and where do you think I got it, off a tree?"

The old sourdough's eyes bugged out. He shook his head and stared, and then shook his head again. "That's a deer, all right! Can't argue about that!"

I waited for him to congratulate me. I knew that I had shot the finest buck the island had seen in many a day. But De Young said not another word. He seemed almost insulted that a cheechako, a tenderfoot, should have had such remarkable luck. He didn't even ask me to stay the night with him in his cabin, just went out and silently loaded the deer head into the skiff.

I admit I was disappointed at the moment. But in the long run I can truthfully say that nowhere have I known such a staunch, cheerful, strong-hearted group of men as these miners and prospectors who chose a life of loneliness and hardship, and lived it uncomplainingly.

Many a person's hard times can be dismissed as a direct result of their own weakness, carelessness or lack of ability, but in the Northern country, other forces often "broke" a man, beat him down and destroyed his best-laid plans. Unpredictable Nature was the chief force that played tricks with a man's hopes and dreams; but the sourdoughs took whatever came their way, never asking nor expecting sympathy—and rarely getting it!

I remember one old fellow who was justly termed "Hard Luck Lucky." It seemed that some malignant force dogged him and planned special miseries for Lucky. He had twice lost his entire grubstake while shooting the rapids, and escaped with only the clothes on his back. Once he had been marooned for three days on an ice floe up in the Yukon country. He had been attacked by a pack of wolves, and lost three fingers in the bitter battle. He had stumbled on a rich vein of gold in a secluded mountain valley and just as he was about to stake a claim had fallen down a crevice and broken his hip; before he could get back to the claim, someone else had located on the vein, and milked it dry. Lucky had won, and lost, over eight thousand dollars at faro. He had once been offered 25 thousand dollars for a claim he owned, which experts thought would bring in half a million; he had refused to sell, and within days, the vein petered out!

Lucky was both the joke and the admiration of every man in Southeastern Alaska. We wondered at his doggedness, we laughed at his stubbornness, but we were determined, when disaster should strike us, that we would not be weaker than Lucky. We would take whatever came, like men!

Lucky's one driving ambition was to hit "pay dirt" and come out of a claim with enough money to buy drinks for all the boys. He knew and loved every blear-eyed old prospector up and down Southeast Alaska with a brotherly love, and he wanted to share something with each and every one.

One winter's day we were all gathered in Jake's roadhouse, when Harry Jonas, one of the miners, brought us news of Hard Luck Lucky. He had been found by a couple of surveyors far back in the mountains, his back broken from a terrible fall down a half-opened mine shaft. They carried him out, as he babbled incoherently about his "big strike" that would really "pay off this time!" He believed in his delirium that he had discovered the dream of his lifetime, a vein of rich ore.

No one told him the truth. They carried him on slings to our settlement, where one quick look told us that Lucky had a very short time to live. In spite of his agony, he demanded to be carried to Jake's roadhouse. A call was sent out for all the old sourdoughs on the island who had known Lucky during his prospecting days.

They came to the roadhouse and clustered around Lucky on his pallet. "I've done it, boys! Bet you thought Hard Luck Lucky would never hit, didn't you? Well, it's just the richest strike since the Yukon rush! And it's all ours, boys! Ain't no need for one man to keep it all to himself! It's all ours!"

The old sourdoughs mumbled and shuffled their feet. They couldn't believe that Lucky was at the end of his rope. Then, his eyes glazing over, Lucky croaked out his last wish: "Harry Jonas, you're my pal. You've been my partner. Stand the boys a round for me, Harry. I'll pay you back when the strike comes in."

We all waited. We doubted if Harry Jonas had more than $30 in his pocket or in the world. Whatever he had would have been earmarked for a grubstake for himself. And we knew that Lucky's great strike would never, could never, come in.

Harry Jonas didn't bat an eye. "Sure, Lucky. I'll stand 'em a round for you. Your credit's good with me!"

He nodded to Jake. "Set 'em up for everybody!" We drank. We toasted Lucky—and his gold strike. As his eyes filmed over for the last time, we heard him breathe: "That's a partner, Harry!"

Without a word, Harry Jonas put his hand deep into his ragged pants. He drew out 28 silver dollars, and looked at them a moment.

"Tote up, Jake," he said.

Jake figured up the drinks. "Twenty-nine dollars, Harry. But listen, you don't need to—"

Harry clanged the 28 silver dollars down on the polished counter. "I'll owe you a buck, Jake. Mark it down."

He turned and strode out of the roadhouse. It was the least he could do for his old friend and partner. And it was Hard Luck Lucky's last chance to stand a round for the boys.

V

"Medicine Man"

I remember my first disappointment when I arrived at Ketchikan and learned that in the southern part of Alaska, the Eskimo did not flourish. I expected the parka-wrapped tribes with their dog teams, igloos and seal-oil lamps to inhabit the entire territory, and I was greatly disturbed to find out that Indians lived in the southern region. Indians, indeed! Why, I had seen Indians in Michigan, for my home state was once part of the hunting grounds of the mighty Iroquois nation.

Tlingit totem of the Kyan clan, Ketchikan, about 1900.

47

But after I had spent a few hours in Ketchikan, and walked past its strange, towering and grotesque totem poles, I began to take a new interest in these Indians of the North. Later, after I settled down on Prince of Wales Island, I had more time to make a study of them, to learn their habits and tribal customs, and to make friends with some of them as well.

There are three main tribes in that region, the Tlingits, the Haida, and the Tsimsians. No two tribes spoke the same language or dialect, but they communicated through the use of a common jargon called Chinook.

Chinook Jargon was a real, living language, developed in pre-historic times and used all over Alaska and lower British Columbia. In large part it was the descendant of the language of a once powerful Indian tribe that inhabited the lower Columbia River region of what is now Washington and Oregon, plus later words adapted from French and English. Chinook has no grammatical structure, no conjugations and no declensions, yet with all its crude simplicity, there are elements of strength and a picturesque beauty to it.

The word cheechako, for example, which I heard so often, is an everyday word in Alaska. *Chee* means "now," or "new," and *chako* means "come"—a perfect tag of contempt or good-natured derision for the newcomer, to set him apart from the honorable title of sourdough, or old-timer (a relative term, since traditionally it referred to someone who has seen at least one break-up of ice in the Yukon).

Cultus is another commonly used term from Chinook, ranging in meaning from merely useless to so bad as to defy description. A cultus fishing stream is a disappointment to the fisherman; a cultus souvenir is probably some cheap trinket; a cultus man is a good-for-nothing.

The Chinook phrase *Saghalie Tyee*, on the other hand, is as charming an expression as any lover of picturesque English might

48

Early Metlakatla, Annette Island, Alaska.

desire. That which flies high goes *saghalie* (upward, over)—that is, a bird, a cloud, a wisp of smoke; and *tyee* is the boss or chief. Therefore, *Saghalie Tyee* is the big boss who flies high above the trees and above all others—that is, God. (*Tyee kopa Washington* would be the president of the United States.)

When I went to Alaska, at the turn of the century, a group of some 800 members of the Tsimsian tribe in Canada had recently been given exclusive rights by the United States to an island just south of Ketchikan, where they founded a self-governing, self-sufficient municipality, which is still flourishing. The Tsimsians owe their good fortune largely to the devotion and to the efforts of Father William Duncan, a ruddy-cheeked Scot who spent his life amongst them as their spiritual leader. A lay priest in the Anglican Church and a strong believer in native rights, he rebelled against the rulings of his own church and against the authority of Canada, which did not at that time grant aboriginal rights or citizenship to its Indians. Father Duncan petitioned the United States to help him establish a colony for his followers. The result is their town of Metlakatla, laid out along the lines of "Old Metlakatla," a town they had founded in Canada 25 years before their exodus. "New Metlakatla" holds stores, a sawmill, a church, and many business enterprises, run by the Indians themselves.

I had the privilege of meeting Father Duncan when I visited the Tsimsians' remarkable model village on Annette Island. I asked him what flag the Indians acknowledged.

He replied with a twinkle: "Look at me! My cheeks are red, my hair is white, and my eyes are blue. That is flag enough for them!" And so it seemed to be.

One of the first souvenirs one is offered upon disembarking at Ketchikan is a beautifully woven basket or hat, presented by a woman of the Haida tribe. I greatly admired their basketry, and bought several examples to ship home to my family in Michigan. The workmanship was so handsomely done as to make me curious about the Haida Indians.

The Haida in the old days were a very powerful tribe, noted for their long, graceful war canoes which could make raids as far away as Puget Sound. Besides being famed canoe makers, the Haida carved small totems and statues from polished slate-stone, inlaying the figures with shell. They also wove their baskets and hats, waterproofing the twined fiber and inserting intricate designs, usually executed in black or rich red—a human ear, an oyster shell, or the head, wings, tail and webbed feet of a duck. Like most of the other Alaskan Indians, the Haida often wore nose and lip rings, a mark of distinction.

It was Garness who first introduced me to the Haida village of Howkan, on Long Island, near the southwestern tip of Prince of Wales Island. Here stands one of the last great forest-like clusterings of totem poles, those poetic structures carved out of cedar trees which symbolize the Indian's bid for immortality. I used to visit Howkan often, to stand and wonder at the wild primitive faith that could inspire these soaring, distorted figurines, leering down at me from their mighty heights.

Naturally I was much interested in the fantastic poles, whence they had come, what they stood for, and what inspired hand had carved each one. I learned that totem poles are not tall carved images of long-dead Indian gods, as I first thought, but rather records of individual or family or clan events and allegiances, and that although they appeared ancient, they were relatively recent expressions of tribal art.

It was the Tlingits for the most part who inhabited Prince of Wales Island. In the old days, I was told, they painted themselves with vermillion and lamp-black, mingled with oil, but at the time I was in the settlement they had largely taken on the habits of the whites. Some of them were very handsome, particularly the young girls, with shapely figures, bright eyes, red lips and clear skin and strong teeth. In observance of old taboos, some of the Tlingits still practiced the custom of isolating their young women for a considerable length of time, just as the girl changed from a child into a maiden.

I also investigated the great superstition regarding the "shamans" or medicine men. These august personages were accorded great respect, and their supernaturally acquired power to cure was both feared and venerated by the rest of the group. Tlingit medicine men carried with them certain ceremonial masks, as well as tubes made of ornamented bone for blowing sickness away or catching souls. The hair of the shaman was never cut; it was his shaggy mark of office.

The life of the Indians and their tribal customs kept me enthralled, and I spent as much time as possible getting to know the men and their chiefs. This was easy, for we depended upon the

Indians to catch enough fish for all of us at the settlement, and then we would barter for it. The women were shy and for the most part kept to themselves.

Word got around the settlement and eventually leaked over to the Tlingit camp that I was something of a medicine man. Occasionally one of the Indians was troubled with a sore or wound which my basic knowledge could heal, and I was told they wanted very much to come to me for help. But they feared my black medical bag, so eventually it was decided that they would send the Indian foreman of one of the mining companies to try me out.

Alec arrived at my shack one morning, his face swollen and inflamed with an abscessed tooth. I think, however, his fright at being the first victim of the "American medicine man" was greater than his pain.

"Well, let's have a look," I said, as briskly as I could, and seated him on a keg of salt herring. I tipped back his head and motioned for him to open his mouth so I could peer inside at the infected tooth. He gave a squeal of pure terror and leaped up, fished in his pocket, and drew out a small bag, ornamented with tribal signs, which he hung around his neck. This was to ward off evil, he indicated—if I looked into his mouth without this bag around his neck, I might see his soul and capture it.

Now that he was protected by the amulet he was content. I could see that the tooth had to come out; it was affecting his whole bloodstream. But all I had in the way of dental equipment was an ancient pair of dental pliers, or forceps.

I doused him with antiseptic, quickly slit the gum around his tooth with a razor blade which I had sterilized in the fire of a candle, fitted the pliers over the infected tooth, and yanked. It slid out as if it had been planted in butter. I handed him a flask and he took a stiff gulp of whiskey.

Through it Alec never twitched a muscle. He spat blood a couple of times, and then rammed his finger into the hole. A grin spread over his face. I had passed the test as a shaman.

He fished again in his pocket and drew out a crumpled dollar bill. He handed it to me, and I thanked him, quite earnestly. It was the first medical fee that I ever earned.

I fitted it away in my battered billfold with a sudden twinge of regret. Was this to be the beginning and end of my medical career? But before I could devote too much time to the thought, Alec plucked at my sleeve. To further prove his admiration and devotion he wanted me to accompany him salmon fishing. I needed no second invitation. I went!

VI
The Lemon Pie

The first year I was in Alaska, there was so much to do and see and learn that the days slipped into weeks, and the weeks rolled by from month to month, until my birthday marked almost a full year of work and adventure in the north country. I was tearing the calendar page for March off the slightly lurid cardboard calendar I had tacked up in my shack when I was reminded that April 12 was my birthday. I had first set foot on Alaskan soil the spring before.

Birthdays call for a celebration, and I determined that in spite of the difficulty in getting supplies I was going to make my Alaskan birthday memorable with my usual birthday treat: a lemon pie!

Downtown Ketchikan, about 1904.

Mother was a superb baker, and to my way of thinking she concocted the most delectable lemon pie any boy, or man, ever put into his mouth. Her pies were thick, with a foaming white frosting. The frosting had been gently browned in the oven, and was speckled with little dots of golden melted sugar. One year when I was quite small Mother said, "Fred, it's getting near your birthday. What kind of cake would you like? I'll make any kind you want, and put some candles on it for you."

I considered only a moment. Cake was fine, but then there was that lemon pie. "Well, Mother, the cake I would like most is ... a lemon pie."

"A lemon pie? That's not a birthday treat! You can't put candles on a pie!"

"You can put the candles on something else, Mother. I would rather have a lemon pie."

Of course I got it. A lemon pie, just tart enough, and frosted over with white fluff, speckled with golden brown.

The next year Mother asked me again. "Son, last year you didn't want a birthday cake. I think we'll make an extra nice one for you this year. What kind would you like?"

"I'd just like lemon pie, if you please, Mother."

She never asked me again. Each year, my birthday was marked by the baking of a large lemon pie.

So my one thought in faraway Alaska was to celebrate my birthday appropriately by baking a lemon pie for myself. There were only two drawbacks to this ambition: I had never baked a lemon pie, and I had no idea where I could get any lemons.

My first stop was the supply store on the island. The storekeeper and I were old friends by this time. Everyone on the island bought their supplies from him, and my mining company ran a bill with him from month to month.

"Lemons, Jake—any fresh lemons?"

He just looked at me and laughed. "Where do you think you are, Loomis? This ain't Florida, y'know!"

"What about a boat? Any coming in?"

"No boat, and no lemons. How about oranges? Got a few left. Kinda wrinkled, though."

Orange pie for my birthday? No. Lemons. It had to be lemons. I thought to myself that if I had to hire a boat all the way to Seattle I was going to have lemon pie for my birthday. It's funny the obsessions that can take hold of a man when he has lived alone for a period of time.

I had a little launch, so on the day before my birthday I climbed in it, cranked up the prima donna motor, and sputtered off for the mining center, more than 60 miles away. Spring days in Alaska are often raw and windy, and on this certain day a breeze was kicking up the waves, so strongly that my trip resembled a rollercoaster ride.

Success awaited me at Ketchikan. They had lemons! And fresh eggs—always a delicacy in Alaska. While I was stocking up, I remembered that the mine foreman had asked me to get dynamite, so I loaded a ton of the stuff into the launch along with everything else.

It's a fact that you can be blown just as far with one stick of dynamite as with 2,000 pounds, but that didn't calm my nervous system any. I was riding on a sleeping volcano, as the nose of the launch pointed back toward Prince of Wales Island.

The breeze quickened, and the waves were rougher now. The small boat bobbed and ducked and tossed around on the crest of the big swells like a bottle cast afloat. The tightly packed dynamite began to shift around. I was torn between hanging on to my rudder and trying to dodge the big waves, or going after to steady the boxes of explosive.

Then another thought struck me: the eggs! If I broke the eggs I couldn't make my pie! So the remainder of the 60 miles homeward, my mind was too occupied with worrying about the eggs to be disturbed over the shifting dynamite.

The storm continued to increase in fury. The next day, the day of celebration, a howling north wind shook the cabin and wriggled through its cracks in little icy gusts. The rain slashed down in torrents. I was delighted. No work in the mines on such a day. I could stay home, in my snug little shack, and bake my lemon pie.

Carefully consulting my well-thumbed cookbook, I decided I could manage the lower part, or pie shell. It seemed to be merely a case of mixing flour and shortening and a little water and salt in the proper ratio.

Beginner's luck was with me. I stuffed the iron stove with wood to make a bright steady fire, and baked the shell. It came out perfect—gently browned, firm and flaky. Then for the filling—here was the hard part!

As I took out my precious lemons, I remembered watching Mother. She grated her lemons till they were kind of bald, and she used the shavings from the lemon peel to flavor the pie. But I didn't have a grater.

However, the code of the frontier specifies "if you ain't got it, make it," and I set about doing just that. I fished out a used evaporated milk can, a hammer and a big nail. (In Alaska, we used canned milk altogether because it was impossible to get fresh milk into the remote regions.) I sliced off both ends of the can, leaving just the cylinder of tin. Then I found a sturdy round of firewood that would fit nicely inside the can, and slipped it through. I laid one end of the wood on a chair and sat on it, and braced the other end on another chair. Then with the can firmly braced on the wood, I began hammering holes in the can. I worked down a row, then spaced another row about half an inch from the first one, and so on, pounding the nail through each time. I thought grimly that if anyone peered in at me, busily pounding holes in a can, they would think the lonely life had affected my mind. And it wasn't an altogether funny thought. Lots of men went "snow crazy" in Alaska.

When I finished pounding holes, I cut down one side of the can and hammered the edges till it was flattened, then ran my hand gently up and down the rough points on the other side of the tin. I now had the most beautiful lemon grater you can imagine!

I shaved all my lemons, just as I remembered Mother doing it, on my milk can grater. I separated the whites from the yolks of the precious eggs and whipped them up, then added the other ingredients, including the squeezed lemon juice, and finally the strands of lemon peel. The topping came out very well, and I dotted it with flecks of sugar, hoping they would melt to the little drops of golden brown I remembered so well on Mother's. After I slid the topped pie into the oven, I waited nervously for it to bake, like a schoolgirl at her first cooking lesson.

About 20 minutes later I lifted my masterpiece out of the old wood stove. It was, if I say so, as beautiful a pie as I have ever seen. Now I wondered how it would taste.

No birthday is complete without a few friends to wish you happiness and congratulations. I had invited Garness, of course—not telling him the reason for the special invitation—and I also asked Ben, the old prospector who months before had almost frozen to death when he could find no wood at my shack. We had become good friends in the meantime.

Ben was always a wonderful guest. He had a lively imagination and could tell the most fabulous stories of any man on the island. He claimed to have been a drummer in the Civil War and insisted that he had heard President Lincoln deliver the famous Gettysburg address, though he always insisted it was made at Shiloh. We never told him differently.

About seven in the evening, the two of them stomped in like great, wet black bears from the forest, wrapped as they were in furs and skins, blowing and puffing.

"Well, Fred boy—what's the occasion? Giving away your vittles?"

I smiled. "Thought it was time we had a party, fellows."

Ben snorted. His straggly beard quivered in indignation. "Party? You don't think it's a party, with no women! Where's your women? Do you furnish them, too?"

"Not this time, Ben. But I've ordered in a dinner—special from Delmonico's in New York. Sit down."

Garness and Ben muttered appreciatively at my birthday table. I had cut up one of the sheets Mother had sent me to do duty as a white tablecloth, and I had raked some spruce branches and pine cones around a lantern for a centerpiece.

Then I proceeded to serve them steaming deer steaks, taken right off the rib, with french fried potatoes, delicious gravy, and thick black coffee—a fine Alaskan meal.

We all ate with lusty appetites, and when the platter was, so to speak, licked clean, Ben leaned back, undid his belt and hiccuped with evident relish.

"Boy, you outdone yourself! That's the finest I've ate since I marched through Georgia with General Sherman!"

"I shouldn't think you would have eaten so well then, Ben," I needled him, and winked at Garness. According to my history books, the Army of the Grand Republic had fared pretty hungry on its sweeping invasion of the South. But far be it from me to contradict Ben.

"Fine eating, Fred!" said Garness. "Mighty fine."

"Just hold your horses, partner," I said. "You ain't seen nothing yet!"

I stepped into my little kitchen alcove and lifted down my birthday pie. I had mounted it on a piece of cardboard box with holes punched all around the edge, and rammed the candles left over from Christmas through so that when I lit them the lemon pie was encircled with blazing pinpoints of light.

59

Then, like a head waiter with the *piece de resistance* of the meal, I marched to the table bearing my pie, enthroned amidst the flaming candles.

Garness and Ben were stupefied. They just stared, mouths wide open.

Finally Garness said, "In the name of heaven, Fred, where did you get it?"

"I made it. All by myself. I went 60 miles to get lemons and eggs and toted 'em back with a full load of dynamite—and if this pie isn't as good as it looks, I'm going to swallow a stick of that TNT!"

Ben was overcome. He kept shaking his head and repeating, "It ain't true. It ain't true!"

But when we sank our teeth into the pie, we knew it was true enough. It was delicious, right down to the last crumb. And you can be sure that last crumb was reached in double-quick time.

When we had thoroughly scraped our plates and licked our chops for any lingering traces, Garness and Ben sang "Happy Birthday!"—slightly off-key, but plenty loud and earnest enough to warm the hearts of all. Even in Alaska, I had spent a very happy birthday, complete to the last detail: lemon pie!

From Edith Loomis' diary for Thanksgiving 1904:
"F. cooked turkey for DeYoung, Shaffer, Garness and self.
Mr. Burkhart gave it."

VII

Pay Dirt, Porcupine Stew, and a Mail-Order Bride

By the time a year had passed plus a few more months, I was convinced that the future was uncertain for the company's scattered claims. I returned to Michigan to make my report and recommended that some of the mining claims be abandoned and that only enough work be done on the others to retain possession, until they might show more promise. Before I left Michigan, my father and I sat down for a long talk.

"Son, what are your plans? You've had a year in Alaska—I should think you would have adventure out of your blood."

"It's a great territory, Dad! A place for young men, strong men! It holds so much promise that I feel I would like to go back."

Frederic Loomis, right, and fellow sourdough.

"What about medicine? You've already dropped behind your class. In a few months, your classmates will be accredited doctors."

I felt a twinge of regret. My classmates—the boys I had studied with, joked with, explored the mysteries of the microscope and dissection and anatomy with—would soon be doctors! And I— what was I? A bookkeeper, an amateur prospector, a laborer for hire. For a whole year my head had been filled with such questions as: "Shall I hunt today, or go fishing?" "How much gold tonnage to the square foot of rock quartz?" Were these the thoughts that would sharpen my brain for a life of medical service? For the first time, I almost wavered in my lifelong ambition of medicine. It was so easy to just let things slide. My father's voice brought me out of my reverie.

"I know that you still have travel in your blood, Fred," he was saying. "And I know it's partly my fault that you're not in medical school. But I would never forgive myself, or you, if I didn't know that sometime, some way, you'll get your M.D."

I reassured him, and as I spoke reassured myself. "I will get my M.D., Dad. You can depend upon it. But in the meantime, I will go back to Alaska—for one more year."

Little did I think that the "one more year" would turn out to be six!

It was agreed upon that I was to return, but not on the company's payroll. I would work by the day as a common miner, at miner's wages, and in my spare time look after company interests.

With excitement and high hopes, I set forth again for Prince of Wales Island. Mingled with my eagerness was the knowledge that I was returning not as a despised "cheechako" but as a sourdough.

The whole gang at the settlement were there to welcome and greet me. I felt that now I was one of them, a seasoned veteran of the great north.

There is always the fascination and adventure of frontier life—of one's own cabin, snug in the wilderness, of deer meat and bear steaks, of duck and geese and ptarmigan hunting in season, and of salmon and trout and halibut fishing ... and in addition to all this, the chance that any day might uncover the glitter of the gold that lurks in the rock.

The newcomer to the mining fields is attracted first by "colors," the streaked rocks that yield evidence of precious gold as part of their makeup. But the seasoned miner knows that "colors" can be panned in almost every stream, and that even in a vein of rock quartz, much of the gold is not "free" but is chemically combined with other, useless rock. To get at such gold, stamp mills are needed to crush the ore, and the concentrates must be shipped to far-away smelters to extract the valuable and leave the dross.

Because in so many cases the gold is mixed together with worthless rock, much of the gold found is not worth the time and money it takes to extract it. By the time it is blasted loose, stamped into chunks the size for shipping, and sent to the smelts, it has cost more than the value of the metal. Many an old miner has spent his life stumbling onto gold veins in the rocks, only to find the vein isn't rich enough to warrant "working" it. And so he travels from place to place, from claim to claim, hoping, always hoping that someday he really will hit "pay dirt"—ground rich enough to pay off.

Garness and I joined this hopeful little company looking for the hidden glitter, the tell-tale flash that will make all their struggles and hardship worthwhile at last.

We knew what we were in for. We knew we would find "stringers"—fine veins of gold in the rock that pinch out so quickly. We knew we would stumble on "pockets" that shine like bright jewelry boxes, only to disappear in a few inches of blasting. We knew we would hit, time and again, the mysteries of the "footwall" that is sure to be rich "when we get a little farther down." Yes, these are the lures that tie the prospector to his search until his clothes are rags, and his supplies of flour and bacon and Arbuckle coffee and Log Cabin syrup are gone. And then he must work for wages again, until he can save up a small "stake"—and then off he goes, following the dream.

Gold is found in Alaska through two different methods. One way is "quartz" mining. The other is placer mining, or panning— that is, put simply, scooping up the rocks and silt from the bottom of a stream or river bed, and sluicing off the dirt till nothing but rocks remain in the pan. Then those rocks are eagerly examined to see if there is a trace of "pay dirt," which is to say, gold. When a miner finds a spot where several nuggets of gold are yielded up by the stream, he considers that he has a valuable strike, and then he will settle down from his wandering to "work" it, and see if it pays off in a worthwhile amount. Usually he diverts the bed of the river, and channels it away from the section of bedrock which he thinks to be valuable; then he sets to work with pick and shovel to scoop it up. He builds himself some sluice boxes, with water spilling down to wash away the dirt and leave the valuable nuggets behind to be sorted and weighed. In southern Alaska, where we were working claims, the ground is not always frozen solid, and usually a pick and shovel can tear away the riverbed. But farther north, the ground and riverbeds never thaw. There fires must be built, to thaw out the ground enough to sink charges of dynamite for blasting, so that hunks of the earth can be torn away. After the blasting, the rock-like, icy pieces of riverbed are stacked till spring, at which time they are sufficiently thawed to place them under the sluice boxes, to wash them and search for gold.

Quartz mining, the other method of looking for gold, simply means sinking shafts in a hill or mountain where a vein of gold is believed to run, and picking and dynamiting out hunks of rock. These hunks are sent to the smelting plants, and melted down for the valuable metal. Usually companies are set up to undertake quartz mining, for much equipment is needed, plus regular transportation; but in the case of placer mining, a solitary man can usually wring a miserable living out of the streams and riverbeds, by constantly panning for gold.

This was the life that Garness and I cut out for ourselves, and in this way the seasons flew by, with fluctuating fortunes. As we made a little profit we would sink it—literally sink it—in holes in the ground, and in tunnels 50 or 100 feet long in solid rock, pursuing phantoms.

The lesson was brought home to me, time and time again, why old-time prospectors are called "sourdoughs." It is because, half their lifetime, in the extremity of their poverty, they exist on sourdough biscuits, the cheapest and easiest way to fill a hungry stomach. Now that I no longer represented "management"—that is, the company that dominated the mining interests on the island—and had become, in truth, a sourdough like the rest of the fellows, I found myself entering into a delightful new period of comradeship. Miners are a loyal lot (except perhaps on New Year's Eve—I will say more on that).

Garness and I had some strange neighbors for friends. Even a small camp is never too small to hold the unusual. Across the creek from me there lived an old man named Verne, who had built himself a snug, secure house—not just a shack, covered with "shakes" as ours were. Verne had laid a foundation, and planked his floor with split log planks, and roofed his home with shingles, every one of which he had hewn out by hand, himself.

Verne kept insisting that he was not a miner at all, although he went out with pan, pick and shovel every day. He said he was only in Alaska because his little sloop had been wrecked. We used to kid him and ask where he was going in his boat when it so conveniently smashed to pieces on the shoals off the island coast.

"Oh," Verne would say, with a perfectly straight face, "I was on my way to them Hawaiian Islands. But doggone it, I got blown off my course a little!"

Verne was a veteran of the Civil War, and each month he received a small pension from the federal government. I remember that he almost kissed me when he found out that the famous battery in which he had served was commanded by a half-uncle of mine who bore the same name as I.

It was from Verne that I received my first Alaskan recipe for cooking. "You take a medium-sized porcupine, see, and throw it in the pot with a good-sized stone. Boil it till the rock turns soft. Then you drain off the water, throw away the porcupine, and eat the stone." For some reason all the miners on the island thought this was an exceptionally funny joke.

Almost next to Verne's neat little house was the odd-looking shack of my friend Ben, who kept insisting he had been a drummer in the Civil War. Ben had built himself his cabin out of unfinished lumber, but strange to say he had never put in either a door or a window.

When asked about this peculiar omission, he always answered, "Shucks, I ain't going to ruin these four walls for the guy who buys it!"

"Who's going to buy your house, Ben?"

"Well, I don't know yet. But I might want to sell it someday, and the guy who buys it might not like where I've put that door and that window!"

And for all the years that I was on the island, Ben used to enter his house through a loose board in the floor, using a candle by day and night to cook and eat by.

Across the trail from Ben was the strangest character of all. Jesus Junior we called him, for he was a quiet, studious fellow who trimmed his beard and hair to look like pictures of Christ. He read theology all the time, and he belonged to a sect that denied that the world was round. No amount of argument ever had the slightest effect upon him.

"But J.J.," we would argue. "What about sailors who take a voyage around the world? How do you explain it?"

"Thee seest it not," he would answer quietly, placing his fingertips together in a prayerful attitude. "These deluded ones merely skirt the border of the great plain upon which we all live and work and have our being."

"But the sun, J.J.? It rises and it sets. Doesn't that imply that the earth revolves around it?"

"The sun is a great orb which circles the table land, called Earth. Study the Scriptures, and thee will see it is so."

He insisted that at the Second Coming, which he thought might take place any day, such unbelieving eyes as ours would be opened to the great Truths which he understood, and we ignored. None of us quite understood how Jesus Junior lived. He seldom received mail, and he never was seen to work in the mines. Occasionally in the summertime we would come upon him, clothed in a long woolen robe, picking huckleberries along a forest trail. Most of the time, however, he must have lived on the Truth.

Charlie Markle was one of my best friends, a young, well-set-up chap of about 26. Charlie was as rugged and untamed as the wilderness in which he had grown up, for he had been brought to Alaska at the age of 12 by his father. His father was killed soon afterward in Sitka, and the youngster was left to fend for himself. This he did quite well. He learned to prospect and hunt and fish like a man, and when he grew to manhood he commanded a good living as a guide for hunting and prospecting parties.

One day Charlie came over to my shack bursting with a great secret, which he had to share.

"What now, Charlie? What have you done?"

"Fred," he began, a bashful grin spreading all over his honest, open face. "I've ordered a wife for myself."

"You what—?"

"A man gets tired of washing his own socks, and cooking his own grub. And I figured it would be awful nice to have somebody to talk to."

"Go on, boy, let's have the rest of it."

Charlie reached inside his heavy lumberman's jacket and drew out a tattered magazine. It was the pulp adventure variety, and on the back page I read the lurid advertisement, "WHY LIVE ALONE? LOVE CAN BE YOURS! JOIN THE LONELY LETTERS CLUB AND FIND HAPPINESS!"

"I didn't think it could hurt anything, so I wrote. See here—" He drew out of his pocket an ill-scrawled letter on a piece of brown wrapping paper. "This is just a copy. I wrote it off neat. And I sent along her passage, too. She's coming up from Seattle."

I was horrified. But how to tell Charlie that he had been hoaxed? I shuddered to think what creature would get off the next packet boat.

"But Charlie—didn't you even ask to see her picture? Do you know what your wife will look like?"

"She's a sight for sore eyes, is what she is." He dug deep into his whipcord pants and drew out a wrinkled picture. I could make out two women standing together; one middle-aged and weighing I estimated 300 pounds, the other a trim, pretty blonde-haired girl of perhaps 19.

"See here, Fred. It says on the back it's Mary Sue and her family. I reckon she means that's her mother."

I peered at the writing on the back of the picture. Well, everything appeared to be in order. I only hoped that my friend had bought himself a good-hearted as well as good-looking wife.

For the next few weeks, Charlie was in a fever. He spent over

$500, half his life's savings, buying materials to "fix up" his cabin. He laid in a supply of food to last the entire winter, and outfitted himself in the best "city slicker" clothes he could obtain, for the wedding. The rest of the miners and prospectors on the island had a gala time, kidding him half to death, but Charlie was so proud of his "boughten" bride he didn't care.

The steamer came in from Seattle on October 15th. Charlie was to meet the boat at Ketchikan, marry his Mary Sue, and after a week's honeymoon in Ketchikan bring her back to the island. On the eve of his departure for the port we threw a stag party for him.

I went down to the wharf to see him off in his launch. In his heavy whipcord pants, high-laced boots and red flannel shirt he was a fine figure of a man. I knew, too, that he was a good man. I hoped his bride would appreciate his virtues.

The next morning as I was frying flapjacks in my shack there was a thunderous knock, and my door flew open. It was Charlie, wild-eyed, covered with salt water spray, reeking of rum. Since he seldom drank I knew that a major catastrophe must have befallen him.

"Charlie! What's the matter? Where's your bride?"

"Don't ever mention no bride to me! I've been hornswoggled for sure!"

I sat him down, poured him a steaming cup of coffee, and dragged the story out of him. The Seattle boat had indeed brought his bride—and her family! Five of them! And the worst of it was, his bride was the hefty matron. The girl in the picture that Charlie had mistaken for his bride-to-be was her oldest daughter!

"Nothing's going to make me take on that bunch!" he stuttered. "I'll head for the woods! Nobody can find Charlie Markle if he don't want to be found! I'll run away!"

"Take it easy. You can't do that. You're responsible for her. You've brought the woman up here, and you've got to do something about it."

Charlie set his teeth. "I'll hide in a deserted mine. I'll live with the wolves. There ain't gonna be no wedding!"

Somehow I persuaded Charlie to head his launch back to Ketchikan to settle the matter, and I went with him. In the meantime, his blushing bride had settled bag and baggage at the Bar O'Gold saloon and had so charmed the saloon keeper that he had made her a proposal of marriage. By the time we put into Ketchikan, she was as eager to get rid of Charlie as he was to shake her off.

So the whole affair ended not only amicably but happily. Charlie was delighted to take second best and marry Mary Sue's lovely young daughter, Sally, who was quite taken with the young woodsman. He brought her back to the island, and settled her into his cabin, and I'm pleased to report that as far as I know they have lived happily ever after.

VIII

New Year's Eve Claim Jump

I soon learned that calendars are not very important in an isolated frontier settlement. We marked the passage of time by seasons—the long winter and the brief summer—but more often by the arrival of the mail boat from the mainland. Mail day was far more of a holiday than the usual celebration days of Christmas and New Year's and Fourth of July.

Mining tramway near Dolomi, about 1904.

The mining camp seldom observed Sunday, not out of any thought of disrespect for the Sabbath but simply that when one is racing against time to work a claim, it is easier to stop for a rest day when the body is exhausted, rather than every appointed seventh day. We usually declared a Sunday on a stormy day, although calendar-wise the day might be a Wednesday or a Friday. Whatever day it actually was, our "Sunday" usually turned into Wash Day before noon. We had no sheets to trouble us, sleeping as we did wrapped in our blankets, but everything else was boiled together in a five-gallon oil can. After a few washings I understood the Alaskan's preference for blue—the blue from his flannel shirts boiled into the other garments and colored them. But better that than the rosy hue from a red shirt!

If Clarence Strait was too rough, even our impromptu time-marker, the mail boat, didn't put into shore. The hours we regulated ourselves, to suit the seasons. During the brief summer, with its long days sometimes holding 22 or 23 hours of daylight, we practiced daylight saving long before it became a household word. We would screw our watches ahead three or four hours and work till we dropped, then sleep like the dead till it was time to return to the mines again.

When hunting or fishing seemed the order of the day, we would shoulder a gun, or launch a fishing skiff, and vanish for hours, sometimes overnight, with no thought of the passage of hours. We ate when we were hungry, slept when we were tired. This timelessness is part of the lure of the frontier life, I think, because man is first of all a creature of impulse. The regularity of habit imposed upon him by the invention of clocks and watches can easily be thrown off in the wilderness.

There is one date, however, which no miner or prospector needs a calendar to bring to mind. That is the 31st of December—New Year's Eve. This is probably the most significant evening of the year to every gold-seeker in the Alaskan north country.

The reason is this: Mining claims in a new district are usually held solely by who got there "fustest with the mostest," to borrow General Nathan Bedford Forrest's oft-quoted expression. In other words, whichever sourdough has declared that a certain piece of land is his "claim" (and is being worked by him) holds possession. Actual title, giving him permanent possession, does not pass to the sourdough until his land has been surveyed, with boundaries laid out and government reports filed.

When all this has been taken care of, a claim becomes actual property and is said to be patented, and then it is rightfully owned. But in a frontier land, where the gold strike was running riot, no prospector wanted to go through all that red tape for a piece of ground that might turn out to be worthless. All the prospector wanted was to hold onto a piece of land long enough to test it and see if gold might lie beneath the surface.

So a new practice sprang up. A man could claim a piece of land and hold onto it, merely by declaring it "his," for one year. But within that year, $100 worth of development work that might benefit the claim had to be done within its boundaries. When the work was not completed or at least commenced by the end of the year, the claim could legally be "jumped" or taken over by anyone. This held good even if the claim had been developed a great deal in past years and neglected for the current year only.

This meant that on New Year's Eve every miner and prospector in Alaska was out either "working" his own claim to protect his title to it or jumping another man's claim that had not been worked. Part of the rule was that if a claim hadn't been worked in a year it could not be jumped by its old owner. The miners got around this ruling by Jim jumping Bill's claim, and Bill jumping Jim's, and then eventually trading claims back again privately during the course of the year.

Before the end of each year, location notices on printed forms were made out, and new names for the claims chosen. This was always interesting. The miners could trace their friends' love affairs by whatever names were given to their claims. What girl wouldn't be interested in knowing that her name was given to a gold mine? It was a standard method of feminine flattery. But what a situation that miner found himself in, at the close of a year, when he was forced to write that someone else had jumped his Susie! Of course, the claim might have turned out to be a total loss in the meantime, and Susie, too.

Carnation milk cans, with which Alaska is littered, were used to hold the location notice. The top was cut partly out and bent inward to hold the paper in place when the can was inverted. Covered by this little tin roof, a notice would remain legible for years, with a piece of ragged paper stuck inside bearing any name from Girl Back Home No. 1 to Local Beauty No. 12! One of the saddest sights in Alaska, I think, is to see a lonely battered tin can sticking upright on a rocky plot of deserted land that years before had been some prospector's dream of gold!

So New Year's Eve was a busy night for the mining clan in Alaska. There was no wild revelry, no horns and kisses at midnight. Theirs was the lonely forest path by which they might stake out a claim before the turn of the year. Little parties slipped out quietly in time to reach their "discovery point" by midnight. Two by two they went, so that the claim jumper might have a witness as to the hour. Softly they padded through trails sometimes half hidden by snow, their swinging lanterns making strange moving shadows in the trees, the silence of the night broken only by the sudden crash of a frightened deer in the nearby brush, or the wild howl of a wolf in the distance.

At midnight there would be a flash of action, and scores of milk cans appeared upside down on scores of trees, each containing a notice that 1,500 feet along the "strike of this mineral-bearing ledge" is claimed by Thus-and-so. And in this way, a claim was officially jumped and could be held for a year. Later the ends and corner posts of the property could be marked, and a copy of the discovery notice filed in the office of the Recorder of the Mining District.

But often claim-jumping led to bitter tragedy. I have heard many a tale about how brother turned against brother, friends became enemies, all over who had previous right to a claim. When a man has cut himself off from family and companionship, endured loneliness and cold and desperate hardship in the north woods to search for gold, he takes it hard when his claim is jumped on a New Year's Eve.

There were two sourdoughs up on Prince of Wales Island who had prospected together for years. Garness knew them well, and I bunked them down in my shack a couple of times. Joe Winthrop and Barney Cooley had grubstaked all over Alaska during the Yukon rush, and neither of them had ever done more than eke a miserable living out of their placer and quartz claims. They were buddies in every sense. Joe had twice pulled Barney out of the rapids when their kayak had turned over in the dangerous northern rivers. Barney had mushed 50 miles through a blinding blizzard to bring Joe out of a cache where he had holed up with a broken leg. Their slogan was "One for both, and both for one," and their firm friendship was admired and respected by every man on the island.

Joe and Barney would trek down to the settlement, load up on supplies and vanish into the hinterland. Sometimes they would be gone for months and establish dozens of claims, working them like gold-hungry beavers until they proved worthless. On one of these trips into the back country, Barney had separated from Joe overnight and stumbled into a hidden valley. There he had run against a gold vein that looked fairly good and established a claim that he called "Point Hope No.7."

In the meantime Joe had worked around the territory near their place of encampment and had unearthed another small vein, which he staked out a claim for, calling it "Disappointment Ends No. 1."

Before either of them could exploit the new claims, the winter season came down in all its fury, and they were forced to abandon camp and return to the settlement, to work at odd jobs until spring opened up the trails again to the back country.

On New Year's Eve, however, just as every other prospector was forced to do, Barney and Joe had to trek in to re-locate their claims. They left a week early to allow plenty of time, and it was agreed, as was the custom, that Barney would jump claim on "Disappointment Ends" and that Joe would take over Barney's valley claim, "Point Hope." Then, during the year, they would trade back again.

This was done, and the two old friends returned to the settlement and waited it out till spring. Just when the trails opened for travel again, Barney contracted a malignant fever, and we persuaded him to catch the steamer for Seattle for treatment. Joe was returning to work the claims.

A few weeks later word spread out of the hills: Joe Winthrop had hit a strike! A rugged vein of rich gold ore, deep and wide and high-grade! It was the talk of the island, and excitement ran high. What wonderful luck, and what grand news for Barney when he should return, especially since the gold was found on Barney's original claim, Point Hope.

A few weeks later, just after the first shipment of ore had been made from the Point Hope claim, Barney landed, pale, weak, but jubilant.

"By thunder, we did it! Me and Joe! We've made ourselves rich! I knew one of them claims would yield up!"

One of the old sourdoughs hanging over the local bar taunted him. "Yeah, Barney, that claim yielded, all right! But whose is it now?"

Barney looked puzzled. "Mine, you silly coot. I'm the one who scared it up!"

The grizzled old miner smiled mockingly through jagged teeth. "But who holds the claim on it? Remember? You swapped Point Hope for Disappointment."

Barney's pale face turned deep purple. He slammed his fist down on the bar. "Listen, Point Hope is mine! I found it! Joe found Disappointment, and it's worthless. I've seen empty plots of land before, and nobody's getting nothing but rock out of Disappointment!"

"Yeah, but you're the one stuck with Disappointment, and Joe's got the claim on Point Hope. Looks like you're out in the cold, Barney boy!"

Barney was like a wild man. In a matter of hours he had gathered his gear together and put out his launch to round the island and pack in to Point Hope. His suspicious aroused by the old miner's jibes, his brain inflamed by the terrible fear that Joe would hold out on him, he was beyond reason or control.

Gold changes many a man, and many a principle. It had changed Joe Winthrop. He had forgotten the long years he and Barney had struggled together, the kinship and camaraderie of their great friendship. He forgot that according to their pact he was merely holding Barney's Point Hope claim for him. He thought only of the fact that he had worked it while Barney was away, that he had slaved alone in the dank shafts and suffered the backbreaking labor. He thought only that it was estimated that the Point Hope mine would bring him over $200 a day while it was being worked.

The meeting of the two old friends was like setting a fire to gunpowder.

"You low, thieving rat," grated Barney. "You plotted against me. You told me you'd give me back my claim. You tricked me!"

"I did nothing of the sort. It was your idea that we should jump each other's claim. It was all done fair and square! If the

Disappointment Ends claim had rendered up gold, it would've been yours."

"I'd have split with you, Joe! You know I would!"

"I don't know any such thing! Like as not you'd have kept it all. Same as me! Barney, don't make trouble. I aim to keep the Point Hope!"

"And give me, who found it, nothing?"

"Well, maybe a little something."

They stood on a slight rise of land overlooking the Point Hope— the dark shaft dug deep into the ground, gold ore in plain view. Barney's red-rimmed eyes narrowed. Slowly his right hand crept toward his hip, where his heavy clasp knife was cached. Joe anticipated him.

"No knife, Barney!" he cried, and with a driving uppercut to the jaw he sent Barney sprawling on the ground. Gathering his strength even as he went down, Barney was up and at him like a wildcat. Joe swung again and connected, a bone-shattering hook flush on the nose. Blood spurted, and Barney went down again. This time his fever-weakened body refused to react. He stayed down, gasping for breath and whimpering a little under his breath from rage and frustration.

Joe nudged him roughly with his boot. "Get up and get, you scum! Get off this claim, and don't let me catch you around here again. Next time I'll kill you."

Barney slunk away, but raw murder glared in his half-mad eyes.

All that evening and throughout the next day, Barney stood at the bar in the settlement and drank. He poured down one slug of whiskey after another, and all the while he muttered: "He did me out of what was mine. He was my friend, and he did me out of it!"

The evening of the second day he staggered away from the bar and disappeared into the night. An old harbor rat recognized him in the gloom and asked him where he was going.

"Back to Disappointment!" Barney growled.

Two days later word got through to our little camp that Joe Winthrop had been ambushed and killed, shot through the back.

There was no need to ask who had killed him. We all knew. Quietly the miners formed a posse, for in the frontier country, men must obey the law, and sometimes be the law. We all trekked into the back country where the Disappointment Ends claim was staked out.

As we neared the claim we spread apart. We suspected that Barney would be holed up in the shallow mine shaft, waiting— with loaded carbine across his knees—for us to come get him.

We eased up to the shaft and stopped just short of firing distance. One of the miners, who did double duty as marshal, yelled, "C'mon out, Barney. It'll save us coming in!"

We heard a wild, croaking voice yell, "Friends! I got no friends!" There was a single gunshot. Then silence.

The marshal turned to the rest of us. "I'll go bring him out, boys. Wait here."

In a few moments he emerged from the mine shaft, the body of Barney Cooley over his shoulder. There was a single bullet hole in Barney's shirt, just over the heart.

Nine days after they buried Joe and Barney, side by side on a barren hill, the rich Point Hope vein of gold ran out. One week later, a vein of ore was struck in Barney's claim, Disappointment Ends. It was one of the richest and widest veins of ore ever discovered on the island.

IX

Shipwreck!

As *Garness and I extended our prospecting journeys* back into the interior of the island, it became necessary to travel much of the way by water. As I stated earlier, only the fringes of the shoreline had trails cut through them or were in any way passable. If one wanted to explore a frontier piece of territory, it was advisable to take a boat around the coast and put in at one of the countless inlets or fjords that studded the banks. This was a dangerous procedure in the violent coastal tides, but it was far better than breaking trail through virgin forests for days, and running the risk of losing oneself altogether.

Southeastern Alaska is subject to extremely heavy fogs, which roll in off the northern seas without warning and blanket the whole area. A ship entering a strait or a narrow inlet is helpless if one of these fogs descends, and can end in pieces against the rocks.

On Clarence Strait.

Veteran Alaskans have learned to steer a boat by its whistle, and this was one of the first lessons Garness taught me. It isn't as absurd as it sounds. In a narrow fjord consisting of nearly parallel cliffs two to four thousand feet high, every toot of a boat whistle, or the tin horn croak of a smaller boat, is tossed back as an echo. As the sound wave hits one rock wall, it bounces off and is deflected against the opposing wall, thereby making two echoes of one. The trick of keeping your boat in a straight course when locked in fog is to keep these two echoes simultaneous. If one echo is heard by the man at the wheel sooner than he hears the other, he knows he must veer to the other direction until the sounds are equalized. Then he can be sure he is in dead center in the middle of the channel.

In many places these towering cliffs, overhanging a narrow waterway, are unbelievably sheer, both above water and below it. The knife-like granite peaks climb straight out of the icy depths—and try as you might, half the time a plumb line won't reach the bottom of the water. On one trip I tied the launch up to a little bush clinging to the side of a cliff that reared straight up for over 4,000 feet. I feared that the falling tide might land my boat on a submerged rock, so I dropped a line over the side to take the depth. The line didn't hit bottom. Since it was fairly long—200 feet or more—I became curious as to just how deep this fjord might be. I played out a seine line, and finally this line, too, gave out. It was extending downward 2,000 feet and still I hadn't hit bottom, only eight feet from the shore!

One raw March day we put out from the settlement to sail up the northern shore about 80 miles for some assessment work. Mr. Burkhart, a fatherly old man who helped run the grocery store in the settlement, had invited Garness and me to accompany him in his own fine new launch. He was also taking Isaac, a tall, strong Native from the village, who often accompanied us as hunter and guide.

As we loaded up the launch with heavy equipment and supplies Garness observed that the gray sky foretold heavy weather.

"She'll take it all right!" said Burkhart proudly, indicating his new launch. "She's as snug a little lady as ever I saw."

"Burkhart thinks more of that boat then he does of his wife!" joked Garness, and we all laughed, because Mr. Burkhart's devotion to his sweet, motherly little wife was well-known to everybody on the island.

"Mother wanted to go along to break in the boat, but I said better not. It's pretty rough on the open water this time of year."

"It's murder!" I said and shivered. I did not relish the 80-mile trip in the open boat.

Finally we lurched out of the harbor in the little boat. She was indeed a snug little vessel, and her heavy load served to keep her steady in the violent water. But because of a heavy cross-wind, we did not make good time, and darkness overtook us when we were still some miles from shore.

Garness consulted with me worriedly. "Think we had better ask Burkhart to let us take over? The old man doesn't see so good."

I hesitated. There was no worse insult than to suggest a man wasn't able to pull his own weight or handle his own business.

"Burk's a good man. He can put us in, Garness. Let him alone."

"I don't like it!" Garness gasped as a heavy wave hit the little launch broadside, lifting us for one terrible minute and then hurling us down into a pit of raging water. "It's black as pitch out there, and Lord knows where he's heading us. If we run up against a rock shoal we'll have to swim for it!"

Isaac's stolid face paled visibly in the gloom. He made a motion as if to ward off evil, and muttered something.

"What's the matter with you, Isaac?" I yelled, for now the fury of the wind was increasing.

"Isaac not seal—not fish! No swim! No swim!"

We both stared at him in dismay. These Alaskan Indians lived on the water, practically since birth. They eked out a living fishing for halibut and salmon. It had never occurred to us that they might not know how to swim.

"You no swim?" I shouted back at him, over the wind.

He shook his head and, wrapping his arms about his body, hunched his shoulders to indicate cold. Of course! I thought. Who would choose to swim in these waters, frigid the year round? Although the lakes might be somewhat more hospitable, the sea could well be deadly to someone trying to learn to swim.

Suddenly it seemed to me that in the past few seconds the wind had noticeably increased its angry velocity. Body bent against its curving force, I struggled aft to the tiller, where old Burkhart was crouched, jockeying his craft through the water.

"Have you got your bearings?" I roared.

His face clouded. Cupping his hand, he yelled back at me. "Should be off shore just about now. But how can I put in, in this?"

I recognized his problem. The little bay we were heading for was narrow, hedged in with sharp shoals and great promontories that could rip the bottom off a far sturdier boat than ours. If we foundered, and were hurled into this buffeting sea, none of us would glimpse land again. We would sleep this night, and forever, at the bottom of the ocean.

Then I heard Garness shout, "Heads up!" and I looked just in time to see a wall of water, poised above us, ready to strike. In that split second before the monster wave came down on us with the force of a pile driver, I had the sense to grab a stanchion and hang on. The water struck, and as the launch plunged down, down into the hideous vortex, I felt it grind against a rock.

Then brine washed over us, powerful fingers of water ripped at us, and with a violent motion the launch was hurled upward on the crest of another wave, more gigantic than the first.

"Over the side or we'll founder!" screamed Garness.

My heart recoiled from his command even while my head accepted it. We were on the shoals in the midst of a raging storm. The launch was so loaded that another wave like this one would drive us hard into the rocks and bash the bottom in. The only thing to do was to lighten the boat, hoping that she would clear the rocks. If we lost her, we were lost, too. If we could float, and hang onto her sides, maybe we could last out the storm.

"Out! OUT!" bellowed Garness, and I could dimly make out his shadowy figure dragging at Isaac's arm. Isaac resisted, and Garness again tugged at him. Then, as another towering wave began to roll us up onto its dreadful bosom, Garness swung a pick handle. It caught Isaac alongside his ear, and he dropped in his tracks. Garness caught him as he slumped and in one fluid motion heaved the limp body overboard—then knifed after it, before it hit the water. I swiveled to see what was happening to Burkhart. He was lashing the tiller so the launch wouldn't pitch away from us in the boiling surf. He cheeks were wet, and not from the salt spray.

"Jump! Jump, man!" I cried, and jumped myself, straight out into the black water.

The shock was agony. The water was liquid ice, and as those frigid waves closed around my body I thought for one wild moment that my muscles had frozen solid. Every nerve was a pinpoint of pain, crying out against the cruel cold. But the mind miraculously takes dominance when the body loses its power, and somehow I found myself kicking my feet and breaking the surface of the sea. In the darkness, the launch was a black object against a black sea. I shouted, and from a few yards to my right came a feeble answering shout. It was Burkhart, his face a white patch of terror. I realized that his old bones could not withstand this chilling water. I flailed over to him, and grabbed his collar just as he was sinking. Once my fingers closed around him, I felt that I could never move them again. They seemed to freeze in place, curved in a grip on the old man.

I shouted again, my puny voice swelling up in the raging gale, and from somewhere in the dark sea I heard a faint cry. Garness! Then I made out a shape, clinging to the side of the launch and trying desperately to swing it toward us. It was Garness, holding to the boat with one arm and gripping the limp form of Isaac with the other.

I will never know how the four of us survived the ensuing hours. Isaac finally regained consciousness, and we all clung to the sides of the launch as if we had grown to the gunwales, rising with the boat on each surging wave and steadying it as it fell into the shallows between combers. Our bodies were pounded and buffeted by driftwood that swept in from the open sea; the fury of the lashing salt waves lacerated and burned our skin.

Twice during the nightmare I thought Burkhart would lose heart and let go the gunwales. I knew that if one of us turned loose it was the end, for no man had the strength to pull a companion from the icy waters. Isaac was moaning—a dirge, I fancied, to some northern god—and his cries against the background of the screaming wind and the crashing water sounded like a weird symphony of death.

Some time toward midnight the tide turned, and almost as if signaled by a mightier power the storm quieted. There was nothing to do but hang on to the boat as it rode on the crest of the tide flow and beached itself on the sand. We fell beside it, sodden, stiffened figures of misery. I thought I should never rise again.

It was Garness who saved us all, Garness of the steel muscles and the heart of a lion. He dragged himself up from the beach and staggered to the launch. With a mighty effort he heaved himself into the boat and began throwing out sealskin-wrapped bundles and packets of food and clothing.

My own manhood was challenged. I hauled myself over to help him, and soon Isaac followed. We unlashed a blanket roll and swathed Mr. Burkhart in it. He sat like a frozen mummy, teeth chattering, his hair rigid with salt like a stiff halo around his head.

"Quick!" cried Garness. "There's a bottle of whiskey in my blanket roll. Open it up and give him some."

With ice-bound fingers I tore open the blanket pack. The stench of raw spirits hit me full force. In the buffeting, the cork had come out, and the entire contents of the bottle had soaked into Garness' socks and blankets. It was one of the saddest moments of my life.

Isaac and I struggled to pitch a tent in the dark. Then we set up our sheet iron stove, working for over an hour with trembling fingers before we could fit the pieces of stove pipe together. Garness was already in the woods that bordered the little strip of shore, hacking away with ringing ax at a spruce.

Isaac found bits of dry wood, which we needed for tinder, in the crotches of old trees. Using the miner's trick of laying a candle across the top of the wood in the stove, so that it would melt down and burn as the little flames licked up from below, we finally had a fire.

We brewed coffee, and beef tea to give us strength, and there in the raw cold we stripped to the skin and huddled around the fire while we searched our blanket packs for dry clothes. Poor old Burkhart had a terrible case of the shakes, and we piled clothes on him till he resembled a fat old sea walrus. Finally, more than an hour after we had beached the boat, we were ready to curl up in our blanket rolls and sleep away our horrible experience.

I'm sure that if such an adventure had befallen a city man, he would have died from the exposure. But so hardy were the four of us that when we awakened, hours later, we had only stiff joints to mark our experience. None of us suffered any further ill effects—not so much as a cold!

Even Burkhart's launch would have been in good order except that a 50-pound anvil had broken loose and smashed half the gasoline connections as it lashed to and fro and pounded against the sides of the boat.

After a day's rest, Garness and I left Isaac to care for Burkhart, and we rowed 44 miles in the little skiff that had been attached to the heavier launch, to summon help to tow Burkhart's boat home.

Our shipwreck served for exciting conversation for about a week, and then it, too, faded into the vast store-house of memory. In Alaska, men find new adventures with every sunrise. They have little time to dwell upon those that are past.

X

The Hands of Murder

Partnership in the isolated north requires an unusual amount of patience, forbearance and understanding; for when two men are together day in and day out, under all sorts of conditions, the smallest thing can cause a break that may result in grim tragedy. Alaska is full of such stories, of sudden outbreaks, violent hatreds, carefully nurtured grudges, deep-laid plots, all committed by men one against the other who were at one time finest friends.

Frank Conley and Bert Lawter had worked together punching cattle in Arizona, had jumped the border to laze through Mexico, had sawed timber in the great north woods, had run a saloon together in brawling, booming San Francisco. What was more natural than they should pool their cash to grub-stake themselves for the gold fields of the Last Frontier? They invested in $3,700 worth

"Through a Glacier Window"

88

of supplies in Seattle and embarked for Ketchikan, where they added a third to their prospecting company, Thad Hanlon, a so-called guide and mining consultant.

The three of them packed into the interior. They were young, hardy men, true frontiersmen by choice and by temperament, and the tough, grinding haul toward the frozen Yukon Territory they accepted as just another adventure.

The first few days out were without friction. The three men alternated pulling the supply sledges and breaking trail, and took turns chopping wood and unlashing the supplies when they pitched camp at night.

Frank and Bert swapped stories with their new friend, Thad, around the campfire, jibed at each other, and grumbled good-naturedly. Their spirits were high, their tempers were good.

Along about the fifth day, Bert was breaking trail. Frank was straining under the rawhide thong of the supply sled, which dragged behind his taut body, a dead weight. The snowdrifts were deep and mushy. Going was easy over the packed trails, because with the constant passage of many feet and sleds, the snow would pack down into a firm, glassy road bed. But as suggested by Thad, the guide, the three were using a cut-off, across virgin snow.

Suddenly up popped a giant snowshoe rabbit, and Bert veered off to shoot him without first calling a warning to Frank, who was tugging away, head bent down. Unwarned as he was, Frank floundered into a tall snowdrift and sank to his waist.

He struggled up, furious.

"You crazy galoot!" he shrieked. "If you're going to break trail, break it!"

Bert turned aside Frank's fury with a laugh, and the incident was ignored. But it remained a small pinprick of irritation in Frank's consciousness.

Later that evening, when the three pitched camp, it was Bert's turn to cook. All three men were starving, and their mouths fairly watered at the prospect of the large, juicy rabbit that Bert had shot.

While Frank was unloading the pup tent, and pitching it, and unstrapping the bed rolls, he thought with increasing delight of the hot fried rabbit for supper. As he turned away from his chores, cold, stiff, tired and ravenous, he looked up just in time to see the skillet, with the neatly quartered rabbit, slip and spill into the blazing open fire. Bert had neglected it for only a moment, while he helped himself to a nip from the flask of rum. Only a moment—but that moment ruined their hot supper for the night.

Frank was beside himself. "You good-for-nothing deadweight! Can't you do anything right? I wish I'd left you in Seattle!"

"Simmer down, boy!" drawled the careless but ever good-natured Bert. "You wouldn't be here if you had left me behind. Half this grubstake's mine, y'know!"

That reminder was adding fuel to the flame. Frank could not refute the truth of Bert's rejoinder, so he lapsed into a sullen silence. Thad watched the two partners, and said nothing.

The next morning it was Bert's turn to foray into the woods, and chop down a supply of firewood for the breakfast fire. While he was out of earshot, Thad approached the silently furious Frank.

"Listen, partner—why'd you get linked up with someone like him? You'n'me—with what I know about the gold fields, we could make a killing. You called it as it is—that Bert is dead weight!"

Thad's words rang in Frank's brain. He had begun, after the night's rest, to feel like something of a traitor to his partner, Bert, and to think that he had been unfair. But with Thad urging him on, his resentment flared again.

"You think he's holding us back?"

"I know it, partner. Listen, I've been on a lot of treks—seen a lot of 'em fail because of a deadbeat like that one. Why don't we just ditch him, and go on alone?"

Frank was shocked. Ditch Bert? Ditch his partner, his friend, his pal of long years' standing? Run out on him in the middle of an Arctic winter, in the middle of nowhere? Just then there was a shout. Bert came limping through the snow, leaving a trail of blood flecks on the white expanse.

"Hey, fellas, look here! My ax blade turned and I drove it across my ankle. Gimme a hand!"

Thad eyed Frank meaningfully. It was just as he had said: Bert was a deadbeat. He was holding them back. With ill-concealed disgust, Frank finished off the wood chopping, while Bert tended his foot. After breakfast they mushed on, their pace slowed due to Bert's limping.

By the end of the day tempers were thin. Their bodies were dog-tired, their patience had run out. Bert was in an agony of pain, the result of trying to keep up. Thad had needled both Frank and Bert alternately all day long, and Frank was exhausted from doing double duty. The going was tough enough without added effort when one member of the team couldn't pull his share.

When they pitched camp that night on the smooth surface of a frozen river, Frank picked up the ax and marched off to the spruce thickets to chop, leaving Thad and Bert to break out the camping supplies and the bedrolls. Thad vanished into the trees. He had stirred his little cauldron of hate and resentment well; now he had only to wait and watch it boil.

Almost an hour later, Frank staggered back, bent nearly double under a load of logs and branches. As he approached the camp, what he saw was enough to start a fire of anger in his veins. Bert had made no move to unpack the supplies and make ready for evening meal. He had simply broken out his own blanket roll, curled up, and now was snoring away, dead to the world, huddled by a large round hole cut in the ice pack by earlier travelers so that buckets could be let down for water.

As Frank emerged from the trees on one bank and started out onto the ice, Thad, who had been watching from the other bank, came forward.

"Thought I would go try to bag some fresh game for supper," he called. As he neared Frank, he said "Bert said he would make camp, but I see he hasn't done a thing!"

Frank dumped the logs off his back. He moved directly over to the huddled shape on the ground and nudged Bert with a violent toe. Bert groaned and struggled up, out of sleep, on one arm.

"What's—what's the matter? Supper ready?"

"Supper! You sniveling goldbrick!"

Bert looked up into Frank's contorted face. "What's eating you? Thad told me to take it easy. Said he would get everything ready."

Frank shot a look at Thad. Thad shrugged as if to say, "A liar, too!"

Deliberately, Frank walked over to the supply sled where his Winchester rifle was lashed to the top. He yanked it out of its casing and snapped it into readiness, walked directly back and stood beside Bert.

"Now then. I'm done with you. I'm going to kill you right here and shove your lazy carcass down that ice hole. They won't find you till spring!"

He leveled the rifle. Bert said nothing—just stared at him with perplexed, level eyes. But Thad, who hadn't figured on this turn of events, crumbled. He leaped at Frank and shoved the gun up into the air, as it went off with a roar.

"You gun-crazy? Don't kill him! Just throw him out, and you'n'me make it alone!"

But the explosion of the gun, and the sudden awful realization that he had nearly murdered his best friend, sobered Frank. He stood still for a moment or two, heaving and panting with the force of his emotion. Then as his head cooled and reason swept back over him, he took a long look at Thad. He peered into Thad's squinting, greedy eyes. He looked back at Bert's calm face.

It dawned on him that Thad was playing him for the biggest sucker of all time. Thad intended that he should get rid of Bert so that he could cash in on their grubstake. He remembered Bert's slashed ankle and his uncomplaining trek through the snow all day long. He thought back to the trail of blood, lacing the white with red.

"Bert—say it again. What did Thad tell you?"

"I said it once. He told me to take a rest, he'd make camp."

Frank rammed another shell into the Winchester and swung slowly on Thad. "You've been the cause of this whole thing. Take your gear and get. This is the end of the trail with us!"

Thad stood still a moment, measuring his man. Then something in the set of Frank's stern face warned him that the wisest thing he could do was put miles between himself and Frank Conley. The next time there would be no one to knock the rifle out of Frank's hands.

On bitter Alaskan nights, when the wind rages around the walls of lonely shacks, when men gather to share each other's solitary hours, they tell many tales such as these. I had heard them, and wondered at them, and only half believed them, until the time came when I, too, knew what it was like to hate—and try to kill— my best friend.

Garness had warned me that sometime during the course of our prospecting partnership, no matter how attached we were to each other, no matter how close our interests lay together, we would find we could no longer bear the sight of the other, nor stand the sound of his voice.

One autumn we were working on a discouraging claim about 75 miles in the middle of nowhere, surrounded by wilderness and faced with defeat. Garness and I had been shut away in this isolated section of the island for weeks, laboring from dawn till dusk trying to make the claim pay off before the winter season came down on us and put a stop to our labors until spring.

Aside from our own voices, hoarse with fatigue and boredom, we heard only the thunder of the sea, beating endlessly against the granite cliffs. Ahead of us, day after day, we saw only the unyielding wall of rock that spelled failure.

A succession of small events, no one of them important, brought on an attack of surliness in Garness. One morning I had burnt the sourdough biscuits; the next day I snapped the handle on his favorite pick. Garness in turn had a habit of hanging his dirty socks over our wood stove, to dry them out. As the steam penetrated through the sweaty wool, the stench was terrible! Also, the good-hearted woodsman's table manners were atrocious, and although I was no Lord Chesterfield, his habit of picking his teeth and spitting while at the table set my nerves on edge.

The days dragged on. Each morning I would rise already tense and irritated, my body taut with the necessity of holding in bitter words and unjust accusations. I could tell by Garness' brooding silences that the same tension was eating his nerves raw.

The claim we had worked so hard and so long was yielding nothing. It was obviously a total loss. But with the stubborn pride born of defeat, both of us refused to give up and write it off as a bad venture. We worked on, sinking new blasts of dynamite into the bare rock, picking and hacking at the shattered blast remains with dull, automatic gestures.

One morning at dawn I turned out of my blanket roll, a red band of pain tight across my temples. Momentarily blinded, I groped for the pail of water we set each night in the embers of the fire, so that the water would be warm for washing and cooking at breakfast. My unsteady hand caught the pail at a crooked angle. It tipped and spilled, half-drowning Garness as the water gushed out.

He woke with a gasp and a sputter and glared murder at me as he mopped his face.

"I'm sorry," I grated, and I knew in my heart I wasn't sorry at all. Then, a moment later, "Garness, let's quit—give it up. This claim is dead. Let's head back to the settlement."

Garness did not answer me. He snorted contemptuously and walked away, as if I was too much of a weakling to bother speaking to. I seethed inside. I knew that the same question had been on his lips for days, that only his stubborn Norwegian pride kept him from suggesting we head for home. A moment later I could hear his steel drill chattering into the rock.

A little later, after I had downed a bitter cup of coffee, I followed him up to the quartz slab where we were drilling. As I approached, his drill glanced off the rock, sending a shower of broken shale raining down on my head.

I cursed him. Slowly, calmly, choosing my words for their impact, I called him every foul name I could think of. He didn't answer, just stared at me with heavy eyes and fumed back to his drill.

We worked sullenly for awhile, each trying to ignore the other's presence, each seething with injustice, each racking his brain for the worst possible thing he could say.

A little while later I threw down my pick and fetched my ax, and began to hew timber at the foot of the dump. Garness was still working near the mouth of the tunnel. Suddenly, without warning, he appeared at the edge of the dump, holding the heavy steel drill in his hand. He spat out the bitterest insult I had ever heard, a masterpiece of wrath and animosity, the result of days of vicious planning.

It was too much. Every fiber of decency and restraint broke within me, like floodwaters that have crushed the gate holding them back.

I hefted my ax once in my hands and started up the bank. The only thought in my head was to kill—to kill Garness—to carve that square Norwegian head of his into two with my ax blade!

Emotion choked me. My muscles jerked and jumped in their casings of flesh with the intensity of my hatred.

Above me stood Garness, spraddle-legged, drill upraised in his Herculean grip, poised to crush my skull with its weight the moment I should stand level with him.

For a dreadful endless moment we stood, reason, humanity, mercy drained from our faces, the lust for murder etched in horrible lines. I'll never know why I didn't swing my ax, or why Garness never dropped the steel drill that would crush out my life.

We stared for a long minute, the minute that measured our lives, and then the mask of hate washed away and we were men again.

Trembling, I put down my ax gently on the ground and looked at my hands. I turned them over and stared at them—hands that once I had promised myself would be used only for healing, and helping other human beings, and now in a moment of madness had come so perilously close to being hands of murder!

XI

The Gentler Touch

I had a number of friends among the Indian families, but perhaps no one was closer to me than Sitka Charlie, a Tsimsian, who scraped together a living as fisherman, hunter and guide, both on the island and on the mainland. Sitka Charlie and his wife, Mary, had seven children, ranging in age from one to eleven.

The older children attended the small mission school in Ketchikan, and after I knew them better they persuaded me to visit their school. It was a simple little one-room affair, but the children who attended it seemed bright and eager, and I found myself looking forward to other visits when I had business in Ketchikan.

One day Tom Jenkins, the young Episcopal minister in charge of St. John's church and the school, dropped by my cabin on the island for a brief talk.

Edith Prichard Loomis

St. John's Episcopal church and St. Agnes Mission, Ketchikan, about 1904.

"Fred, I've been watching you, and I think you'd make a better schoolma'am than a prospector."

"What on earth are you talking about?"

"Well, the situation is this. The schoolteacher is leaving for the States to get married, and my wife and I are going back to Boston to bring my wife's younger sister out here to take over the school. But that'll take quite a time—six months, I figure. In the meantime, what will happen to the school?"

"Can't you just shut it down? It's been my experience that all kids, Indian or white, like a vacation."

"Yes, but here it's different. If you get these little Alaskans out of the habit of going to school, they'll drop into their old habits of hunting and fishing and we'll never get 'em back to class. I'd like to have you take over the school and run it."

I thought about it a while and decided that it might be a wonderful thing to do. I needed the extra money the job would bring, and Garness and I were at a point where he could get along without me during the week. Besides, I had become very fond of the children.

"All right, Tom. I'll do it!"

Tom Jenkins grinned. I had a feeling I hadn't heard the end of his proposition.

"That's great—just great, Fred. And I'll tell you what: I'm going to let you play preacher into the bargain!"

And so it was that I found myself standing beside a blackboard all week, and in a pulpit on Sundays.

On the weekend that Tom Jenkins and his wife were to arrive with the new schoolteacher, I was called away to the back country on business for the mining company. The next day, when I returned, I hurried bright and early toward the church and school house. As I neared the church, I could hear sweet, melodious strains filling the crisp air. Someone was playing the little pipe organ. Someone whose touch was firm and strong and sure, not fumbling as mine was. Someone was making the most beautiful music I had heard in all my years in Alaska!

Quietly I eased open the door to the church and stepped inside. In the dusky gloom I could see a slender form bent over the keys and pedals, mingling the tones of the instrument into a soaring pattern of melody.

When the glorious music had finally quivered to a stop, I coughed gently. The young player spun around, an expression of surprise on her face. I don't know what she thought of me, the intruder, but I know that I thought she was beautiful!

"I'm sorry. Don't stop. Please go on playing," I said.

"It's a lovely piece, isn't it?"

"Yes," I agreed. "It's lovely." But the song wasn't the only thing I was thinking about at that moment.

"I was just waiting for Mr. Loomis to arrive, so that he could explain to me about the Indian school. Do you know Mr. Loomis?"

I smiled. "Slightly."

"Tom tells me Mr. Loomis is one of the finest men in the area. He was going to study medicine at one time. Too bad he had to give up the idea."

Her words hit me with the force of a blow. Give up the idea of medicine! Why, I had never given up the idea! I was going to go back—finish my medical schooling, win my M.D., set up my practice!

But was I? I had been here ... how long? Two years, three, four? Time had passed me by. My old classmates were already practicing their profession, healing the sick, delivering babies, making calls! No wonder my friends here in Alaska thought that I had indeed given up the idea.

"You look so strange. Have I said anything I shouldn't have?"

I pulled myself together with a start. "Of course not. I wonder if—" Just then the church door flew open and I heard a bellow of greeting down the aisle. It was Tom.

"Fred! Fred Loomis! The old schoolmaster himself!"

Tom hurried down the aisle, hands outstretched, face crinkled in smiles. The girl at my side gave a gasp.

"You—Fred Loomis! Why didn't you tell me—those clothes—I never dreamed—"

I glanced down at myself and ran a rueful hand over my whisker-stubbled chin. Of course, she had taken me for a prospector, a sourdough, in those patched, faded clothes, those dirty boots!

"I'm Fred Loomis, all right. But I wear these miner's clothes as a disguise!"

By this time Tom Jenkins was standing at our side. He gripped my hand, and clapped me on the back.

Edith Prichard Loomis and students, Ketchikan.

"You old sourdough! I'm glad to see you've met our sister, Edith Prichard. I hope you two will get to be great friends."

Indeed we did. I found that my spare time was taken up more and more in Ketchikan, between the Jenkins' home, where Edith lived, and the school house, where she taught. The weeks and months slipped by and soon Edith was no longer a newcomer to Alaska. The words "he had to give up the idea of medicine" returned to needle me in quiet moments, but my days and evenings were too full and busy to do anything about changing my status.

On weekends, Edith and I had become almost inseparable. It was our custom to take my launch up to a secluded little cove about a hundred miles away, and picnic. On a certain day we were anchored in a quiet bay, about 200 feet from shore. Out in the

The mission schoolroom, Ketchikan. ("That the arts of basketry and woodcarving may not be lost, competent native instructors teach the children in those handicrafts." —The Alaskan Churchman.*)*

center of the bay the water is so deep you can't drop an anchor that will hold.

While we were peacefully munching our sandwiches, and talking, Edith gave a sudden start.

"Easy, don't rock the boat!"

"Look, Fred! Look!" She was pointing over toward the shore. I squinted in the direction of her outstretched hand. Out of the woods had shambled an enormous black bear. He was lumbering down to the water's edge.

"Edith, hand me my rifle."

"Oh, don't shoot him. He isn't harming us."

"No—but he'll help us vastly, if we can serve him up in the form of bear steaks. We can use the meat." I snapped the rifle into place and took careful aim. Standing upright in a rocking launch is not

Interior of the rectory at St. John's, Ketchikan.

the most accurate method of shooting a bear. I fired, and the big fellow leaped into the air, forefeet held high, at the impact of the bullet. He reared back on his hind legs, roaring with pain, then came down on all fours and half-sidled, half-loped away into the underbrush at the edge of the beach. I knew that I had hurt him badly but not scored a kill.

I leaned over and cranked the engine into a coughing start. Edith grasped my arm. "Fred, what are you going to do?"

"I can't leave a wounded bear in the brush. I'm going to finish him off."

Edith turned pale. By this time she had lived long enough in the Alaskan Territory to know the danger of tracking a wounded, angry animal in trees and underbrush.

"Fred, please don't go after the bear. If it gets half a chance, it will tear you to pieces."

"But I can't just leave it there."

"I know you don't want to. But if you go after it, I'll be all alone in the boat. I can't start the engine, and we're a hundred miles from home. Suppose the bear does attack you. I couldn't help you—and I couldn't get home."

Women have a way of making an argument so reasonable and so right that there is no answer to it. The thought that I had shot that bear and not finished the job was galling. But there was truth in what Edith was saying.

Reluctantly I started the engine. "All right. You win. But I'll think of that bear with my bullet in him till my dying day."

We were silent for a time, while the launch chugged out of the harbor. Then Edith spoke softly.

"It's not just pride. You hate to think of suffering, don't you? You always want to do what you can to help and heal it?"

"Anybody wants to help suffering and pain."

"Yes, but with you, Fred, it's more than that. I've never seen anyone more fitted for the medical profession. Why don't you go back and finish medical school?"

"I don't know. I'm too old now. I've been out so long."

"You're not too old. In these years up here, you've learned so much. You've matured. I know that these years in Alaska have taught you things that will make you a better doctor."

I looked squarely at her. What was she trying to tell me? Was she urging me to leave Alaska, and therefore to leave her? Or was she trying to intimate that she would go with me—that she would help me, and stand by me, while I began a new struggle? I didn't know, and I was afraid to ask.

"Well, I—I don't know, Edith. I might go back, sometime!"

"It isn't a case of 'you might, sometime,' Fred—you must go soon!"

XII

The Hands of Healing

I like to think that my life has run by pattern—that just as a weaver creates the whole, by twisting and twining each little individual strand, so have I built the web of my days, by recognizing events and occurrences as significant, and therefore acting upon the inspiration they afforded me. Had not Edith come to Alaska, and awakened in me the instinct of marriage and perhaps parenthood, I might not have been so readily tractable when it became obvious that it was time to put away the pick and drill for the subtler instruments of scalpel and forceps. Still, regardless of the fact that one's consciousness toward duty has been awakened, oftentimes it

From Edith's album: "Here you see us in the launch starting out for a long ride. We put up a sail when we started and sailed twenty miles down the water. ... We slept all night on the boat and the next morning started up the engine ..."

takes a dramatic event to push the reluctant will into action!

Late one evening, though it was still as light as noon in the late summer of the North, a sloop tied up at the dock below my cabin. It was blowing a gale outside the harbor, and I knew the little vessel must have been tossed and battered by the sea. In a short time, two tired, rough-looking men appeared at my door carrying their blanket bags. They asked for a dry place to spread their blankets for the night. Visitors in the northern frontier country are always welcome. I had done the same thing more than once, and I invited them cordially in without question, though in another country I should have wanted to call the police. They needed shaves, they were ragged, and they looked like the last remnant of the unredeemed.

I fixed something for them to eat, found a place for their blankets on the floor—the only place I had—and then as we sat down to fill our pipes the rougher-looking one took out his watch. To my amazement the gold key of Phi Beta Kappa flashed from the leather thong that fastened the watch to his suspender button. I wondered where this tramp had found it. He did not have that contented look of a Phi Beta Kappa. He looked more like a train robber.

"Where did you get that thing?" I asked.

"Harvard University gave it to me," he answered. "And it gave me a degree or two, but this tough guy, my partner here, is only a Ph.D. from Yale, and you can't expect much from him. He's nothing but a Greek professor in season, and he's out of season now."

The air was bantering, but they smiled in the annoyingly superior way that seemed to say that in spite of their evident advantages they really did not want me to feel ill at ease with them. I had forgotten that I had been down in a mining shaft all day, and that in my old overalls, faded blue shirt, and sprouting whiskers I looked a great deal like a train robber myself. I was astonished almost beyond speech, but the instant temptation to surprise them in turn was too much for me.

I turned to the tough guy from Yale and very soberly started to recite in Greek the opening lines of the *Odyssey* of Homer. I couldn't have gone farther than those first few lines, but that was far enough.

The effect was all that I could have hoped for. It was their turn to be astonished, and then we all roared and the evening was perfect.

We drew our chairs around the "airtight" stove. Deerskins were on the floor, the great antlers of my famous first buck were on the wall, and over my pine table stretched the 10-foot wings of a bald eagle which I had shot out of the top of a tree, and which had nearly torn my foot in two with the last desperate stroke of its beak. We didn't like eagles in Alaska.

Well-bred but eager questions arising from their surprise gradually drew from me part of the story of my single year at medical school, my financial reverses, my adventurous voyage to Alaska, and the long period of my frontier life. When they asked me how long it had been since I left home, I felt a sudden hot sense of shame when I said "seven years." I realized that I was but little farther ahead than when I might have said "two." Through all those years I had studied fitfully and somewhat aimlessly in a *Gray's Anatomy* which I had used in my one year of medical school. Suddenly the futile years with their cycle of fruitless effort appalled me when I stopped to think what I was, or wasn't, doing with my life.

They in turn told me of the research problems that had engrossed them and to which they would soon return. As we talked, the phantom of the Cap and Gown that ruled their lives enveloped their tattered garb. I saw their cloistered lives and the hedges of convention that I knew their universities placed about them in the academic year. They told me of the absorbing days when together they had planned this trip: to go by steamer to Ketchikan, pick up a sloop, and "just go places"—places where faculty politics and precedence had no part. They loved their vacation and yet it was just vacation, nothing more. For a month they had traveled along the coast, sleeping in their boat, seeing almost no one.

As I watched them, I realized that the brighter gleam in their eyes was aroused not by the present excitement of their trip, but by that same academic life which they had been so glad to leave a few weeks before—to the coming years when they hoped their names would carry authority, when eventually their pupils, reflecting their own personalities, would rise to distinction. Every teacher of advanced pupils has, I think, that same ambition. He likes to see his name on textbooks, even though the royalties are meager. He hopes to hear a leading figure refer to him someday, almost with reverence, as "my old teacher."

The next day I took them underground. I showed them how the ledges are found and traced by their outcroppings on the surface, and how a shaft follows them down or a tunnel follows them horizontally into the side of the mountain. Most of the gold in that district was in chemical combination, but I found a few specimens showing free uncombined gold which they examined excitedly, testing the gold for its identifying softness with the points of their knives. On the way home great flocks of geese in spreading V's honked above our heads, a deer crashed through the brushes near us, and in the stream salmon fought the current and the falls, completing a wonderful day for all of us.

Back in my cabin they hung up their wet coats and put their "gum" boots near the stove, but not too near, to dry. The tenderfoot reveals his status when he hangs them too near the fire, foot-end upward, which makes the steam rise inside the boot to make the foot wetter then it was before. These men knew better.

They dipped water from my rain barrel and washed in the tin

Frederic and Edith Loomis at the entrance to a mine shaft near Dolomi.

basin in the kitchen while I made the eternal sourdough biscuits, cooked venison steaks, and put raw potatoes, thinly sliced, in a covered pan to steam until they were ready to be browned. One never knows how good Arbuckle coffee, then a few cents a pound, can be, until he has tried it under such circumstances.

After dinner we sat down again to talk. I could hardly wait for these intelligent and cultivated men to open again to me the world I had left behind, the little world of classes and students and football and track. Our pipes were going, but just as we were comfortably settled there was a bang on the door. A haggard and bedraggled man whom I had never seen before pushed it open and fell exhausted on the floor at our feet.

I had no whiskey, but I got some hot coffee for him, shocked by his appearance and especially by his eyes, which he tried to shield from the light with his hands. His story came out in broken sentences. He had been prospecting and mining by himself, on the other side of the peninsula. A dozen copper caps an inch long had exploded in his face, and he was practically blinded, and alone. The long, dangerous trip by water was out of the question, so this man had made his agonizing way for miles to my little cabin, partly on his hands and knees, half-blinded, because he had heard there was a doctor there.

I had to tell him I was not a doctor. His face clouded over with disappointment, exhaustion and misery. Watching him, my spirits sank as I thought of my own inadequacy, and then I suddenly remembered that in my amateur medicine case, which had been called upon by all the boys in camp till it had grown thin, there was a little bottle given me several years before, containing a few crystals of cocaine. These had been carefully weighed so that if the tightly sealed bottle was filled, a local anesthetic solution of the proper strength would be made.

"Can't you do something for me?" he pleaded. "The boys said—"

I wondered if I could. I asked the other men to make him as comfortable as possible while I hurried to boil water. I waited for it to cool a bit, filled the little bottle carefully, and instilled the solution in the man's eyes by means of a fountain pen filler, which I had boiled at the same time. Almost afraid to breathe, I touched the bloodshot cornea with a match. He didn't move. My guests from Harvard and Yale hovered in the background, and I forgot that they were there. I was thrilled and obsessed by my first local anesthesia. I looked at my calloused hands in dismay, but I could hardly wait to see what they would do.

It would have been nearly a week before the impromptu patient could be taken on the mailboat across 60 miles of rough water to a doctor. The little sloop had no engine, and a gale had been blowing for days. I felt that the risk of waiting was greater than the risk of trying. For an hour, with the help of the pocket magnifying glass with which I examined rocks, with unskilled but eager fingers, and more beads of sweat on my brow than stood out on his, I dug bits of copper from his eyes. I used a sterile needle and the tip of the blade of my pocket knife, which I had sterilized in a flame. The other men watched, fascinated, without a word, but I was dimly aware that without being told they quietly kept the fire going and a kettle boiling in case I needed more sterile water.

Nature helped me as she has helped me 10 thousand times since. I covered his eyes with boric compresses and we made another bed on the floor. When I had to leave the next morning to do some necessary work, the professor of Greek insisted upon staying in the cabin to keep the compresses moist while his partner roamed the woods. He said he had never been a wet nurse, and might never have another chance even to approximate that distinction. I knew that he wanted to get into the forest which he had come 5,000 miles to see, but he insisted that his new role was just as exciting. Three days passed. We took off the bandages, and the man could see without discomfort. There had been no infection, none of the fragments had penetrated deeply, not one was left, and my first awkward surgery brought me back with a jolt to the thought of the years I was wasting, to the long-deferred hope that sometime I might really know how to do such things and have a right to do them. The man picked up a paper and read as if nothing had happened. When he turned to me and said with a catch in his voice: "Doc, you've given me back my eyes," I hurriedly left the room.

The next morning all three were ready to leave, the miner to do a little work in a blacksmith shop before he returned overland to his prospect, and the Easterners to begin their long trip home. As they finished loading their sloop after saying goodbye and thanking me for my hospitality, I saw them talking earnestly on the dock. Ready to sail, they came back to the cabin. In four or five days, we had become better friends than we could have been in perhaps a year in New Haven or Cambridge, but now they were embarrassed.

"We've been saying some nasty things about you, Doc," the fellow from Yale said. "And that's putting it politely. You've put us up and done everything you could for us, and you know we appreciate it. We watched you forget that anyone else was alive in this whole world while you dug the copper out of that poor guy's eyes. There was nothing the matter with our eyes, though. You didn't know it, but we saw you changed into another person.

"Now, speaking tactfully as one gentleman to another: What in hell is the matter with you? Haven't you got any more guts than to stay here all the rest of your life hammering rock? Don't you know there are other ways of getting to a medical school than sitting on the bosom of your pants, swinging at a drill up here in Alaska? How long does it take you to get some sense? Or are you just one of those morons who doesn't GIVE A DAMN?"

They went away, but there remained the impact of another life upon my own so effective that it started a long train of events quite beyond my imagining. The injured man's recovery and the explosion of emotional dynamite in the tough words of the "guy from Yale" were finally clearing from my mind the half-baked wishes and misdirected efforts that had clogged it for so long.

I saw myself as an automaton! Indeed, the motion of a driller's four-pound hammer, swung at arm's length, becomes almost the work of a robot. The head of the hammer moves through an arc which becomes a groove, a channel in the air. It lands with bone-crushing force, but with practice it lands squarely on the head of the drill that the miner is holding with his left hand almost without attention—almost with his eyes closed—and as the groove becomes fixed, his attention and thoughts are released to go where they may, which is often not very far. The hammer falls five hundred times, a thousand times, perhaps 10 thousand times in a day! A driller's muscles develop until he has a back that looks like a picture from *Physical Culture*, while his brain slowly undergoes the atrophy of disuse, if he will let it, becoming grooved like a worn channel in the rock. Little thoughts slip over it, leaving their little grooves of repetition, and last year's thoughts become again the current of this year's stream of consciousness, finding without effort the paths they have found before. Newer thoughts need newer channels, and the old ones are so much easier.

In a week I had determined to quit, though it would be a year before I threw down the hammer and drill for the last time. I saved the handle of my last hammer, worn into deep grooves corresponding to the fingers that had swung it. I hoped some day I would be able to show it to a son of mine and tell him how his old man had made his way by the sweat of his brow and years of hard work.

Today there hangs on my fireplace in California, where I can see it every day, a fine handmade miner's candlestick still stained with the grease that dripped on it as I used it underground in Alaska. It was pounded out on an anvil, the day he left, by the man who had copper in his eyes. I have prized it always, for I owe him far more than he ever could owe me. Indeed, not his eyes but mine were opened, and I keep his candlestick where I can see it that I may remember with humility the strange turn of fate that led one man to my Alaskan shack, and another back to a medical university.

Frederic and Edith Loomis on their wedding day, January 1, 1907.

XIII

'We Can Do It!'

M*y encounter with the injured miner* awakened old ambitions, half-buried memories of those fascinating days of my medical studies. It stirred up in me a new desire to serve my fellow man through medicine.

But how to proceed? What was the first step to take? I had been occupied for so long now with the struggle for survival on the Alaskan frontier that I was almost afraid to face the so-called civilized world again, and enter the battle of wits in a medical college. Beyond that, if I ever left Alaska, if my dreams of becoming a doctor were ever to be realized, there was one action I knew that I must take. I couldn't go on without a certain gentle, soft-voiced girl from Boston by my side.

We had been seeing more and more of each other, and I believed that I was safe in thinking that Edith felt about me as I felt toward her. But it was expecting a lot to ask a girl to marry you and share hardships for perhaps a period of years—even a girl who had had the courage to come as a teacher to an unknown frontier.

When Edith said "yes," I knew that no matter what happened to my other plans, I had succeeded in winning the one person who would compensate me for all disappointments.

We wrote the Bishop of Alaska, and he promised us that he would come down and marry us in "our" church, St. John's. And so he did. We pledged our vows to the music of the little organ that

*The house at Dolomi. (From Edith's diary, 3/15/1907: "Arrived at Dolomi
a bride of 3 mo. F. just finished cutting wood and not expecting me. Day bright. ...
Garness came up every half hour to see what was going on. Snow."
3/16/07: "First few days F. and Garness stayed home and papered kitchen.
G. as tickled as we over every new arrangement. ...")*

first brought us together, when we had laughed over a case of mistaken identity, and a solemn-faced choir of Edith's students sang at
our wedding.

But in spite of the fact that we were saving our money, and
making plans to return to the States so that I could enter medical
school once more, we couldn't seem to get around to making the
final break with Alaska. As the weeks slipped into months, I felt
myself slipping into a profound discouragement. Was I to become

like so many of the old prospectors on the island, a man who lived in his dreams because he never had the grit to make dreams become reality?

One evening I returned to our cabin, tired, chilled, and very low in spirits. I flung my ax against the side of the table and sank down on the bed as if I would never rise from it again.

"Had a hard day, Fred?"

"They're all hard days. And endless, too."

"Don't be discouraged, Fred. We're working toward a goal. When the time comes, we'll know it."

"Will we?" I snapped. "I wonder. I think you made a bad bargain, my dear. You didn't marry a man with a future. You married a miner who can't get any farther in life than the end of a mining shaft."

Edith was quiet a little while. Then she walked over to me and looked down into my bitter face. "Fred, what are we waiting for? Medicine is the one thing that will make you happy and successful. Let's go back to Ann Arbor. *We can do it!*"

Something in the tone of her voice thrilled me. Her voice was low and calm but very firm. She was sure that I could make a go of it—sure that after 10 years I could pick up the threads of my medical career and go through with my studies. And above all, she had measured the cost to us, in poverty and hardship, and she was ready to stand by me.

A new surge of energy and faith poured through my veins. I shot up off the bed and took her in my arms. Edith said later that my voice rang with a new power.

"You're right! What are we waiting for?"

We started that very minute to make our plans come true. I wrote letters home to my family, to the old dean of the medical school at Ann Arbor. I ordered books and papers and medical journals, and set about concluding my affairs in Alaska. Yes, this time we were going back, for sure!

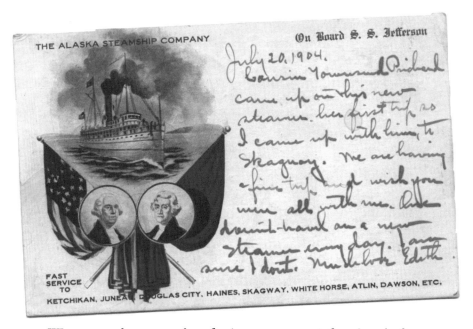

We set our departure date for late summer. A few days before we were to leave, Edith asked me to stop by the school house one afternoon.

There I found her with two of her favorite little Indian girls, bright, sweet, well-mannered, of 10 and 12 years old. Their names were Esther Barton and Annie Lawton, and I think that out of all the many boys and girls my wife taught, these were her two favorites.

"Fred," Edith began, "what would you say if I told you that we were returning with a ready-made family?"

"Family—?" I said. "I don't think I under— ?"

Quickly, Edith explained. "Esther and Annie have begged me to take them back to the States when we go. And Fred—" she hurried on as she saw my face cloud, "I do want to, so much! You know that Esther was able to come to school because she was living with her aunt in Ketchikan, but since her aunt died, Esther's schooling

118

is by no means certain. She's such a bright child, Fred, and so anxious to learn. And Annie, too, could have a wonderful future if she only had the chance."

The two girls looked from Edith to me with shining, hopeful eyes. They loved Edith—loved her as a mother, a teacher, a friend—and through her teaching they had come to know the kind of life they could never have if we left them in Alaska. How could I refuse them?

"You know what this means, don't you?" I asked my wife. "Our money will hardly stretch enough to cover added expense. And besides, think of the responsibility we'll be taking on with these little girls."

Edith smiled. "Fred, we can do it."

So it was decided: Esther Barton and Annie Lawton were to go with us back to the States. After I had given my consent, I looked forward to the joy of sharing our trip with the girls, and their reactions as the wonders of the cities and towns of America unfolded before them.

With mingled joy and sorrow we said farewell to Ketchikan and Prince of Wales Island, our friends there, our home, our activities of the frontier—and hence to Alaska itself! I felt that mine had been an adventure that few had experienced and that still fewer would have the opportunity to know again. For as the orderly civilized world continues to push back the boundaries of trackless forests and uncharted plains and rivers, veiled in mystery, the role of the pioneer fades. I was privileged to be a part of that last great American push into the wilderness, and in a sense I joined the thinning ranks of the last American pioneers.

My farewell to Alaska was in a sense farewell to freedom. I knew that my chosen life of medicine would bring the weight and confinement of responsibility. But that was as it should be.

After the flurry of embarkation, Edith and I settled down to enjoy the boat trip to Seattle. Our greatest delight were our two little charges, who of course had never been on a big ship before. Everything was unutterably wonderful to them, and before the short voyage to Seattle was over, every passenger on the boat as well as the captain and crew had made pets of the two little Indian girls.

Seattle had altered considerably from the rough, brawling town I remembered during the days of the Gold Rush. It had settled into an atmosphere of quieter respectability, and the straight pavemented streets, the modest skyscrapers and the bustling traffic made Esther's and Annie's brown eyes pop with wonder. We took the train at Seattle for a cross-country trip to Chicago.

The girls had also never ridden on a train before—indeed, they had never seen one—and consequently, the ride held a special thrill. They rambled up and down the aisles, swaying good-naturedly with the rock of the train; they stared, fascinated, out of the windows, as the vast American countryside rushed by.

When at last we arrived in Michigan, there were hellos to be said to many old friends, my family was eager to welcome Edith, and we had to make arrangements to place Esther and Annie in a good church school. Then I bent my efforts toward getting a part-time job to support us while I was completing my medical course.

It seemed that we would have almost enough money to see us through. But the next year most of it was swept away for reason beyond our control and I was faced once more with the prospect of giving up school. At the most opportune moment I was offered a place as an assistant in anatomy, which would give us at least partial maintenance. Instead of looking for smaller quarters, Edith found larger ones, a partly furnished house three times the size of the one we had had, and immediately rented enough rooms to students to clear our own heat and light and rent. Even then there had to be scrimping and watching and making things do, patching and mending, turning and remaking her clothes and mine. We lived very simply and had no luxuries, but if she was ever discouraged, she never let me see it. She seemed to know what deadly medicine that would be to a man who was doing his best in a difficult job. As a result, in spite of the rust on my brain, I was a far better student than in my younger, freer days.

At the end of that year, again at the bottom of the bucket, a remarkable job suddenly appeared in which, though not yet a graduate, I was employed during the summer months to prepare a series of illustrated lectures on health and hygiene for the thousands of employees of one of our great corporations. This gave us enough money each year to see us through, with careful managing, till I received my medical degree.

That had been the one goal of years, and we had not thought far beyond it. Again, suddenly, a terrific problem was presented to us. I was offered a place on the staff of a famous teacher, a position that would require four or five years more of university work, with a salary on which we could not live but that afforded an opportunity for a little outside practice. Far more important, it offered training equaled in but few places in the country in the branch of medicine I liked above all others, bringing babies into the world. I did not see how we could do it, but once more it was that girl from Boston who said, "Why not, Doctor? We've made it this far. I've never been so happy—and so proud—in all my life. We are both strong and well. I love it here. We can do it!"

I entered the University Hospital as an intern at a beginning salary of $1,000 a year, which was increased by a few outside patients. I made my professional calls on a bicycle.

A few months later, unexpected fortune struck again. The dean of the department of medicine, from whom stern discipline flowed at times, summoned me to his office. I wondered what ghastly mistake I had made. The dean had known me since I was a small boy in Ann Arbor, but I was more than uneasy when I faced him.

"Fred," he said, "you are about 10 years older than the average student, but you have been one so recently that you know something of their needs; I have heard about all that lecture work you have done on hygiene. We are going to start a Student Health Service and have decided that you are the one to be its chief. You would organize it and would teach. The faculty rank and salary are not settled, but it will be four or five thousand, anyway, to start. It's a big, important job. Let me know right away. Goodbye."

I had hardly recovered my breath when I reached home, as dazed as a buck private who is suddenly to be a colonel. My wife was sitting in the sun, singing to the baby daughter in her arms. The bright light brought out lines in her face that had not been there five years before, but she was radiant and beautiful to me as she looked at her baby. My first thought when I saw her was that this miraculous change in our fortunes would make life so much easier for her.

I told her proudly. The smile faded from her face as if a cloud had come over the sun. Very quietly she said, "Is that exactly what you want to do?"

"Well . . ." I said, a little taken back by her calmness, "what do you think?"

"Why, refuse it, of course," she said instantly. "That's wonderful but it isn't what we came here for. Let's go on as we are. We are not in debt. We're really on our way now, so what's four years more? You'll do best what you want to do most. That's babies, not blackboards!"

Suddenly I had trouble with my voice. Before I could manage the lump in my throat, her smile returned and she spoke again. "And there's another little thing, my dear, if you don't mind too much. I'd like another baby for this one to play with, if you please, sir, and this will be a fine place for that, too."

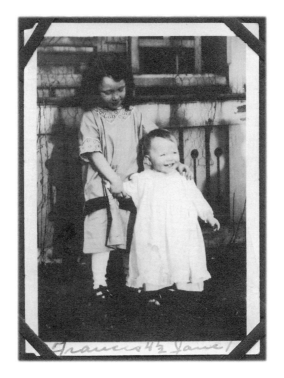

XIV

The Trail Turns West Again

The four years of internship passed almost too quickly. There were thrilling things to tell each day when I came home. Those days, filled with babies and with gynecologic surgery, were often 24 hours long, good training for the man who wanted to be on the reception committee for many more babies later.

Finally, lit to our eyes with the happiness of a thing accomplished and with the spirit of adventure, we determined to make another beginning. Somewhere in California, we decided—we didn't know where. We sold everything we had accumulated except

Frances, 4½, and Jane, 1.

for a few precious treasures, one being my prized possession, the stately old grandfather's clock that had been in our family for over a hundred years. (I have always thought this clock very wonderful. During my early boyhood, if I had been particularly good that day, my father would let me climb on his shoulder, open the glass door, take out the funny little key and wind the clock. I used to want to be good, of course. But it did help to know what my reward would be. It is a strange thing to some, but I think it is a very good example of how boys and girls carry with them all through their lives impressions from when they are small. The two things I remember most vividly: lemon pie for my birthday and our family clock.)

It was October when we set out, in pouring rain, with no notion of where we would sleep that night. But we got in our little auto and started for California. I thought back to that day when my trail had first led me west—when I was just a cheechako on my way to the great Alaskan frontier and the rush for gold. I remembered my wonder and awe at the vast western plains, my delight in the breezy, good-natured western spirit—and I felt that California would indeed be a place where a man could sink his roots, and grow and expand.

For five weeks we drove toward the setting sun, camping and cooking by the side of the road, often sleeping in our car, sometimes driving over lava beds or deserts where at that time there were no roads. There were two small girls in the back seat with their mother—Frances was five years old, Jane almost two. I heard the story of The Three Bears 10 thousand times, I think, always followed at once with "Oh, Mama—tell it again." The bears in all these stories would have reached twice around the world, tail to tail.

We arrived in a little town in New Mexico one night in the midst of great excitement: President Theodore Roosevelt was there to make a speech. I was eager to hear him because I admire him so much and because he had been so nice to me and the other men all those years before. I could still hear his "har-har" when he last saw me, on the old horse that danced backwards along Main Street.

So we all went to hear him, arriving somewhat late, Jane, Frances, their mother and I. It was very crowded and the only vacant seats were right up in front. People don't like to sit in the front row, it seems, but we marched up there. He had started his speech, so we tried to be very quiet and not disturb him. Soon I saw him look at me, and then I thought he was looking at me again. I supposed something was wrong—maybe I wasn't dressed well enough, as we had just gotten out of our car.

Finally the speech was over and we got up. I was so glad to have seen and heard him again. Then to our great surprise he got off the platform and walked straight to our little Jane, picked her up in his arms and sat down with her in one of the chairs. "I don't know you very well," he said. "But, by jiminy, I know your father, and I was talking right at him when I was making my speech. And now I'll give you a good big hug for the Spanish War days. I always felt your father would have made a crackerjack Rough Rider and was sorry he didn't join up with us!"

I do want to tell here what became of those two fine little girls we brought out of Alaska with us.

Annie Lawton was never too strong, which was a handicap at school, so we sent her to friends who had a ranch in the Midwest. She married early, but due to a lung condition that slowly developed she died in her early thirties.

Esther Barton came home to us each school vacation and loved devotedly Frances and Jane, her two foster sisters. She decided early, I am sure partly due to the medical feel in our home, that she wished to go into nurse's training. She became a very fine nurse and today is supervising head nurse of one of the large hospitals in Cleveland, Ohio.

Some 30 years later, after I had made my home in California, she visited us on a return trip to Alaska. She was going there to bring back one of her nieces to educate so she could in part repay the advantages she felt she had received over other girls of her race. She was a fine figure of a woman. It gave me great pride the few days she was with us to take her to Palo Alto to visit my daughter Jane and her "brood" of three, the youngest being about the age Esther remembered Jane when we left Ann Arbor.

Esther Barton and Frances in Michigan.

126

XV

Edith's Account of the Cross-Country Drive, 1916

Transcontinental touring by automobile is no longer the exclusive sport of millionaires. My husband is so far from being a millionaire that a hundred dollars is a matter of gravest importance to us, but we have recently completed a trip from Michigan to California, my husband, myself and two little daughters, at an expense so much less than the cost by rail, considering all we saw and did, that we wonder why even more families are not doing likewise, especially those who are planning to move West permanently. I shall

"We had a new 4-cylinder, 7-passenger car,
costing less than a thousand dollars. ..."

have little or nothing to say of what we saw. It is all so marvelous that I couldn't describe it, and I have long since run out of adjectives. But that a family can make such a trip for the price of an ordinary vacation, in perfect safety, seems too good to be true.

The Car. We had a new 4-cylinder, 7-passenger car, costing less than a thousand dollars. We decided on a 7-passenger model because of the extra room it gave for the baggage, and for the children to sleep and play while under way. My husband is not an expert mechanic, but uses just his ordinary good sense about machinery. He drove this car about 600 miles before we left, to become thoroughly familiar with it, and to develop any inherent weakness or defect in it. Then the agent who sold it to us went over it very carefully with him, as any good dealer will do, examining every bolt and nut, putting in fresh oil and grease everywhere, and spending time enough on it to be sure that things were all right. This took several hours of a desperately busy day, but was worth every minute of it. We saw only too many unhappy travelers on the way who evidently had not taken this trouble, and they paid dearly for it. It was something like accident insurance.

Insurance. We insured the car against fire and theft. This cost $2.25 for each hundred dollars of insurance and is good for a year. We took the insurance in a company maintaining agencies everywhere so that we could get prompt action if necessary. Insurance can be bought at a lower rate in local companies which may give excellent local protection, but we had to think of trouble coming suddenly thousands of miles away. Beware of the automobile of only local fame when you start for distant points. Special prices, personal friendships or other inducements for such cars should be promptly declined. We saw party after party held up in strange places, waiting days and even weeks to have a broken spring or some other part replaced, sending hundreds of miles because there were no big general agencies for their car in that part of the country. And every day of delay meant money, lots of it. The main routes of travel are literally lined with garages except in the mountains and deserts, and the better known makes of cars can be intelligently repaired, if necessary, in hundreds of little towns; but the things that small town garage men tried to do to certain cars with which they were not familiar are too awful to describe. Of course, mistakes of this kind always cost time and money.

The Route. We chose our general route before we bought our supplies. There are several touring associations which publish more or less ponderous books giving exact directions for almost every road in any part of the country. These books give much local information of general interest and are desirable but not essential, and they are rather expensive. We did not have one.

One of the companies manufacturing tires issues excellent and compact free guides which we found very easy to use and, as a rule, accurate. These books direct the traveler to turn right or left at exact fractions of the mile as shown by the speedometer, previously set at zero at a specified point, and it was so fascinating to watch for the turns and twists of an unknown road exactly at the points designated by the speedometer. It makes one feel almost at home and it is almost impossible to lose one's way. This was equally true in making our way through crowded cities or on the long stretches of prairie or desert where, for example, at 2.7 miles we were directed to turn to the left, and at 36.3 miles to "pass house with red windmill," with never a line between. The speedometer really furnished a large portion of the fun and interest, though we never once "speeded."

The main routes across the continent are well marked by sign posts, and some clever genius devised the plan of using distinctive marks on the telegraph poles to show the way. For example, we followed a succession of red, white and blue rings for hundreds of miles along the so-called National Highway without really need-

"It was so fascinating to watch for the turns and twists of an unknown road exactly at the points designated by the speedometer."

ing a guide book at all except to plan each day's run. Nearly everyone knows of the Lincoln Highway, which isn't a separate highway at all, but only a succession of roads which are, or were, the best through each particular area, leading to a definite objective. As each familiar ring or emblem appears in the distance, it is very comforting to be silently reminded that one is not only on the right road but the best one. Sometimes we wondered just how bad the others could be if that were the best, but not often. The roads averaged far better than we expected.

We were ready to leave our home October first. My husband saw several tourist bureaus who advised against the Northern routes or the Lincoln Highway, because it was too late in the year. We were forced to choose the Southern way, by the so-called Santa Fe trail, and have been so glad that we did so. The fall months, October especially, are particularly suited to traveling on the edge-of-the-South way, which is uncomfortably hot, we were told, in the summertime. As the weeks went on, we got more and more to the south, avoiding either extremes of heat or cold.

Equipment. Our outfit was collected with the most careful attention to economy. We bought no special attachments except a "spot light," a movable electric searchlight which is almost indispensable. We used it to find signs and corners in the dark, to cook, read and mend by, and, most important of all, to guide us quickly to the extreme right of the road when suddenly approached by the powerful blinding lamps of another car, recklessly driven. It always made my husband angry to turn meekly aside for such cars, but he did it to "play safe." We decided that the following things were necessary:

Spot light	$ 4.50
One set of tire chains (seconds)	3.20
Two new spare tires	50.00
50 ft. half-inch rope	1.50
Pocket flash light	1.00
1 extra inner tube	5.00
Patches and "dough" for repairs	1.00
Blow-out shoe	.35
Shovel	
Ax	

This list is pitifully small compared to the elaborate lists of other travelers, but it carried us through and incidentally helped many others.

Clothing. To carry our supplies, we had made a light wooden box, 56 inches long, the length of the running board, 10 inches wide and 15 inches high, put together with screws instead of nails, and divided into two compartments by a partition in the middle.

The covers were hinged separately. The box was painted black to match the car, given one coat of spar varnish and bolted to the left running board. The two compartments could be locked separately. In one part I put all our extra clothing, the heaviest at the bottom because we would need that last. In the other part was our kitchen, which I shall describe in a moment. Besides a folding mattress, we took a rubber blanket, which proved indispensable, 2 pairs of blankets, a wool comfort, a woolen lap robe, rain coats and warm bath robes for each of us, including the baby. On very cold nights, we slept in our bath robes and on other nights used them as blankets or pads. The mattress and most of the bedding were carried, tightly folded or rolled, in the tonneau. We found three or four old sofa cushions useful during the day and at night slipped thin white covers over them to put under our heads.

We had several sets of underwear and stockings and one extra pair of shoes for each one. We wore brown poplin or khaki clothing most of the time on the road; our better clothing was carefully folded in a large telescope which was carried easily on top of the wooden box previously described. Our toilet articles and all the things necessary for night were carried in a suitcase, which also rested outside the car on the box. This arrangement, carefully planned, made it unnecessary to do much unpacking each time we camped or went to a hotel.

Overloading. We often felt that we had been wise in deciding against taking the hundred and one things that "might come in handy." We passed many, many cars laboring along with enough equipment for a small farm, carrying heavy trunks, enormous tents, chairs and even bird cages. We traveled for several days with a touring party consisting of four children and the parents, a banjo, a large dog, two rocking chairs and a complete camping outfit all packed into a small car. They had room for all this, but none for extra gasoline, and were about ready to try to vaporize the dog when we came along with the five-gallon reserve supply which we always had ready in a wooden jacketed can, carried with the blankets in the tonneau. We never needed it for ourselves but felt safer to have it.

Food. In one compartment of the wooden box we carried soups, beans, and meat in cans, sardines, sweet chocolate and similar staples. There were days when this compartment was not opened at all, when we happened to pass good stores at a convenient time. When we reached the less thickly populated country, we were careful to keep a reserve supply always on hand in case of a breakdown. We shall never forget a family, including children, which we found in the dark, in an isolated spot on the wind-swept Arizona desert, their car broken down, their lights useless, and without food or water. Only inexcusable lack of foresight can explain such desperate predicaments.

The immediate supplies for each day were carried in a light reed satchel in the tonneau where they could easily be reached for the numerous lunches necessary. We found rolls and buns much better than bread because easier to spread, and because no large knife was necessary. Bread dries so rapidly in the dry and high regions that it is almost impossible to cut it in slices that can be held by children. We used a good deal of sweet chocolate bought by the pound and found raisins and nuts useful between times.

We had substantial breakfasts of ham and bacon and eggs as a rule, sometimes making pancakes with prepared flour. We made extra coffee to fill a large vacuum bottle and usually did not stop for luncheon, at least not long enough to make a fire. We often fried enough bacon in the morning to make sandwiches. While my husband drove, I found it easy to make the sandwiches, and we saved many hours that others lost. We always stopped early enough in the afternoon to find a good camping place and to get things in shape and supper under way, before dark. This is important.

Paper plates and paper napkins were inexpensive and convenient. The latter were used to wash and wipe dishes, too. We car-

"Our cooking was done on a small oil stove when we were near buildings, but in the open we made camp fires."

ried moderately heavy china cups instead of tin or aluminum. If one has ever tried to drink hot coffee from a metal cup, he will understand why. A single frying pan and two aluminum sauce pans proved to be all that we needed. We found a cheap tin coffee pot better and quicker than one made of aluminum for camp use. We saved much time by carrying fresh drinking water in a tightly covered pail instead of stopping each time someone wanted a drink. This pail was set inside a larger pail, also with a cover, to prevent spilling. After reaching Colorado, we got a large water-bag, which hung outside the car and was always cool.

Camping or Hotels. We slept in our car nearly every night. Our front seats were reversible, and by putting the rear cushion on the floor, covering all with an old sanitary couch mattress, our bed was unbelievably comfortable. My little daughter of five slept at the foot and the baby slept in an old hammock which we cut down to the right length and stretched above the rear seat. Even when we went to hotels, she cried for her "own hammock." Even a small car can have the back of the front seat cut down and put on hinges so that at night a comfortable bed may be made. We did not carry or need a tent. A tent is bulky, takes time to put up and take down, and does not give the protection from crawling things that we had, safely above the ground, in our car. When necessary we put up the side curtains but never left them all up during the night. There were times, however, when we would have been glad to have had a small tent for protection from the rain and wind when cooking, and another time we might take one, or at least a canvas fly to stretch out from the top of the car. We met several parties traveling in two cars who put their cars about ten feet apart at night and stretched a canvas between them, cooking under the fly but sleeping in the cars.

Our cooking was done on a small oil stove when we were near buildings, but in the open we made camp fires. Our only stove then consisted of two old bars of iron about two feet long and as large around as a lead pencil. We dug a hole in the ground about two feet long and a foot deep, and built our fire in the hole. It was always easy to find wood, even on the desert. The two iron bars, laid across the hole, supported the frying pan and coffee pot. A camp fire should always be small, especially for cooking, and every old-timer smiles at the enormous fires of the tenderfoot.

Saving Money. Each night that we slept in our car, we not only had the fun and adventure of it, and the buoyant spirits of the early morning after a night in the open air, but also a virtuous feeling of satisfaction in having been paid from five to ten dollars for it, that is, we had saved that much. We went to hotels perhaps once or twice a week when we did not find a suitable camping place, or when we wanted more thorough hot baths. It cost from three to five dollars for our beds alone and averaged about a dollar and a half for supper or breakfast for our party. It never pays to sleep in a second grade hotel, but we saved many dollars by getting meals in clean looking cafes, paying for what we ordered only, instead of paying a very much higher price for the elaborate dinners served in the hotel in which we planned to sleep. I often washed the light clothing for the children in the hotels at night, using naptha soap, and by morning the things were dry.

We frequently asked permission to camp in a field or orchard and were never refused, when we explained that we would have no fire except our oil stove. The farmers and others were interested in us, gladly sold us fresh milk, eggs, fruit and vegetables, and helped us in many ways. Where the travel was heavy, we found our reception even more cordial when we left the main highway and stayed for the night near the first clean and prosperous-looking house on a side road, where travelers were more of a novelty. We were very careful to pick up every scrap of paper or waste in the morning and to thank our hosts for their courtesy. We sometimes found that we could return the favor by carrying some member of the family to the next town.

Information. It paid to ask questions. We learned many valuable things from people on the road and especially from tourists going in the opposite direction about camping places, roads and water. This information was much more accurate than that given by garage men as a rule, perhaps because they were asked so many questions that they were tired of answering. Once when we depended upon garage information we drove 25 miles to find that a bridge had burned and that the ferry was disabled. We had to go back and wait till morning, losing a whole day and traveling 50 miles extra. Another time we were told at the garage that a certain hill was impassable but a ranchman showed us a way around through private roads on the neighboring ranches, saving us a detour of a hundred miles. We found that the local agents for our car naturally took more interest in us and our problems than in other cars.

Maintenance. Every day my husband went over the car, tightening grease cups, seeing that there was plenty of water, oil and gasoline, and keeping the air pressure in the tires just right. This took only a few minutes. In Kansas City we put on the two new rear tires, not because the old ones were bad—they had been driven only 1,800 miles—but as a precaution against annoyance. We drove slowly over rough and bumpy places and on steep grades, and as a result, in part at least, drove from Michigan to California without spending anything for repairs, and, most wonderful of all, we didn't have even a puncture till we were almost on the California line. In one little town in New Mexico, we found six cars laid up with broken springs and axles when we left. Some of these cars had flown by us, over rough road, the day before.

Side Trips. We kept to the main traveled roads as much as possible for convenience and safety. There is beautiful courtesy among tourists as a rule. We were glad to stop and ask if we might be of help whenever we saw a stalled car, not knowing when we might ourselves need help. Our simple supplies were the means of help to many others, and there is so much camaraderie among the modern "Knights of the Road" that wayside acquaintances are part of the value of the trip. Not being in a great hurry, we made side trips to Colorado Springs, the Grand Canyon and to Prescott, Arizona, at amazingly little cost. For instance, the Grand Canyon is less than a day's drive from the main highway. We reached there in time for the wonderful sunset effects and camped only a little way from the rim. There is a magnificent but very expensive hotel, of which we were fortunately independent. I wonder how many families of four have seen the indescribable glories of the Grand Canyon at an expense of four or five dollars!

What It Cost. On leaving our home in Michigan we had in our pockets $216.00, mostly in travelers' checks, which are safe and are honored everywhere. We carried an ordinary check book for emergencies but did not have to use it. We averaged about 15 miles to the gallon of gasoline.

On reaching our destination in Southern California six weeks later, after paying all expenses—this is, having our living for six weeks, traveling 3,850 miles, gaining an intimate knowledge of our country at first hand, enjoying the close companionship of each other for all that time (which is impossible at home with an exceedingly busy husband), and camping in the mountain tops, plains and deserts—we had $22.00 left. If we subtract the ordinary cost of living at home for six weeks from this $194, and the bare railroad fare to California, we can make ourselves believe that we have actually been paid in cash for this wonderful experience. And to balance the wear and tear on tires and machine, which runs now better than ever, we find that the same machine costs just $115.00 more in California than in Michigan on account of freight. This more than covers the cost of tires and wear, we think.

This surprisingly low cost is due in part to good management and careful driving, and in part to good fortune. We were not delayed by rain, sickness or accident as many are, and had no extraordinary expenses. It would not be safe to start West with no provision for accidents or delays, but the hazards can be wonderfully reduced by a little forethought; and the way is made easy by the consistent kindness, courtesy and thoughtfulness which we found everywhere.

XVI
The Greatest Adventure

When we finally reached California, I stopped off in Pasadena to see the only man I knew in the entire state, a doctor classmate of mine. He wanted me to locate there in Southern California, but I had my mind made up for the northern part, so in a few days we were again on our way.

By the time we reached Oakland, across the bay from San Francisco, it was Christmas week. Inquiring around, I found there

North from 13th Street on Broadway, Oakland, about 1913, with
the Cathedral Building (originally Federal Realty Building)
under construction to the right of the Flatiron Building, center.
Photo courtesy of the Oakland History Room, Oakland Public Library.

*Fabiola Hospital at Broadway and Moss Avenue, now MacArthur
Boulevard—present site of Kaiser Hospital, Oakland.*

(From The Peraltan: *"Dr. Frederic M. Loomis, obstetrician, picked up the phone
on the third ring even though it was 2 a.m. He had been sound asleep, and the big
old-fashioned phone with the hand crank hung on the wall in the living room 20
feet from his bed. ... Now he dressed quickly and drove his Studebaker touring car
to Fabiola Hospital ... bounded quickly up the front steps carrying his portable
nitrous oxide gas machine and two containers of gas ... the only such equipment
for use as an anesthetic in obstetrics in the Bay Area in 1917. ...")*
Photo courtesy of the Oakland History Room, Oakland Public Library.

140

was no one in Oakland specializing in obstetrics and gynecology, and so we decided that this was the spot where the need was greatest for the field of my specialty.

I wanted an office by myself where I could for the first time see my name inscribed on the door, FREDERIC LOOMIS, M.D. We selected a couple of housekeeping rooms in a very quiet part of the city, not too far from the hospital. I bought a few pieces of old furniture, scraped them down myself, and repainted and decorated them so that everything would be clean and white and new-looking to start my practice, after the holidays.

With our few remaining dollars we bought a tiny Christmas tree, a few ornaments to trim it, a present for each of us and a doll for each of the girls. I didn't want our first Christmas in our new home, at the start of our new life, to have anything but happy memories.

Almost at once I had patients. The added years of maturity—I was 40 years old by then—and the extra years of preparation made it very easy to get started, easier than it is now, I am sure. In three months we were in the clear, in six we were getting well ahead.

It came almost as a shock to the dear girl whose courage and determination had made all this possible when she realized that there was money in the bank and that she could begin to buy the things she wanted for her small home and her self and her family. Yet this was less important to her than the happiness, expressed almost daily, that the impossible had been "so easily(!)" accomplished, and what fun it had been, and that now her faith was rewarded. And then her first wish was for another baby, "maybe a little boy who some day will want to be a doctor."

Six months later she was suddenly taken ill. It was before we understood the nature of the great influenza epidemic of 1917, the scourge that swept the world, a combination of influenza and pneumonia, deadly to high and low and especially to expectant mothers. She insisted upon arranging the little chairs and tables for

Frances' birthday party, due in two days, before she went to the hospital. The following day she was in desperate condition and in another day, the day of the birthday, with the finest doctors in the city constantly at her side, still smiling as long as she could see, she and her baby died. A true pioneer, she had not been afraid of either life or death.

I recount this now, with emotion that has dimmed but little over the years, to pay tribute to one woman's patience and courage; to say with great humility that those qualities have lived on to lift me to greater effort when other lives have been at stake, and, I think, sometimes to turn the tide; but also to salute the brave women who are fighting on alone with a soldier's fortitude to care for their children left fatherless by the war; to reassure the husbands who fear that their training is coming too late; most of all, to commend and encourage and strengthen the wives who today stand firm beside their student husbands even when hope seems long deferred.

Because of Edith's steadfastness, that first Christmas in Oakland marked the beginning of the greatest adventure of my life, one which has occupied my heart and mind and interest throughout my lifetime—the practice of medicine, filled with drama and the vagaries of the human race.

As I look back on my Alaskan experience I realize that it did not close with a climax, it drew naturally to a termination as my own desires and needs changed. Those years at Dolomi—years of strength, weakness, courage, toil, hardship—were far from lost. They transformed a youth into a man, they supplied maturity from raw inexperience. Leaving Alaska I left friends who had proven themselves comrades in the face of desperate danger and wracking privation. I left the glorious Alaskan countryside, the jagged mountains hiding their secret treasures of gold, the rushing wild rivers, leaping with salmon; the wind-swept clear sea, the brooding forests, sheltering their woodland folk from the hand of the hunter; the rain-gray winters, the mild, blue-heavened summer days.

But medicine has been the dominating interest of my life, a dynamic force that would not let me rest, though I buried my deepest urge for years under the more immediate challenge of Alaska. I feel that I have been fortunate indeed to have had my desire and my destiny blend together so perfectly, to form a life which I am profoundly grateful to have lived, and enjoyed!

My body was made for action. My mind was made for thinking. My heart was made for loving. I cherish these: action made effective by thought and made helpful by love. For this harmony and its profound satisfactions, I thank God too. And I pray for guidance to do a better job tomorrow, if there be a tomorrow.

THE BEST MEDICINE

by Frederic Loomis, M.D.

"IT'S *but little good you'll do, watering last year's crops.*" — GEORGE ELIOT

Dr. Loomis

YET that is exactly what I have seen hundreds of my patients doing in the past 25 years — watering with freely flowing tears things of the irrevocable past. Not the bitter-sweet memories of loved ones, which I could understand, but things done which should not have been done, and things left undone which should have been done.

I am a doctor, not a preacher; but a doctor, too, must try to understand the joys and sorrows of those who come to him. He should without preaching be able to expound the philosophy that one cannot live adequately in the present, nor effectively face the future, when one's thoughts are buried in the past.

Moaning over what cannot be helped is a confession of futility and of fear, of emotional stagnation — in fact, of selfishness and cowardice. The best way to break this vicious, morbid circle — "to snap out of it" — is to stop thinking about yourself, and start thinking about other people. You can lighten your own load by doing something for someone else. By the simple device of doing an outward, unselfish act today, you can make the past recede. The present and future will again take on their true challenge and perspective.

As a doctor I have seen it tried many, many times and nearly always it has been a far more successful prescription than anything I could have ordered from the drugstore.

"The Best Medicine" is the last of many magazine articles written by Dr. Loomis, who died last February 9. At the time he wrote, he knew death was approaching.

From "This Week," San Francisco Chronicle, *April 10, 1949.*

Little Girl Without a Name

"Oh, what luck," a pleasant voice said over the telephone. "This is Anne Skarstad, Doctor. I know you don't usually see patients on Wednesday afternoon, but—well, are you busy?"

"Just about ready to go home," I answered. "Nice quiet afternoon here. Is there something I can do for you?" Anne had been a friend and patient for years and had never once made an unreasonable request, which is more than a doctor can say of all his patients.

"Oh," she said slowly, "I hate to ask you, but there is. My sister came out from Ohio to visit me a week ago with her two children and a helper. She knew that with my two—the two you saw into the world—there would be a lot of looking-after to do, so she asked a sweet girl from the orphanage who had often been in her home as

145

a 'sitter' if she would like to make the trip to California to help take care of all the kids. Of course she wanted to come. She is shy and quiet, but my youngsters love her already.

"My sister expected to stay through August but this noon had a telegram calling her home at once.

"Here's the problem, if that's what it is. My kids began to cry when they heard that Ruthie—that's the girl's name—was going to leave, cried more about her than about their little cousins, really. We've all fallen in love with her. I asked her if she would like to stay and call this her home, and then she began to cry, too—said she'd never had an honest-to-goodness home since her mother died 10 years ago.

"I'd love to have her. She can help me and finish high school and then she is eager to study nursing, I believe. But I hate to take the responsibility of her unless I know her health is all right. Of course I thought of you, and my sister and her children leave tonight, so—well, what do you think?"

I looked at my watch. "Just time," I answered, "if you can bring her right down."

"She's finishing a shower," Anne replied. "I'll get her clothes ready and we'll be there pronto. Oh, thank you, Doctor!"

I could not guess the nationality of the girl when Anne brought her in. She was just developing into womanhood. She had the beautiful dark eyes and skin that suggested the south of Europe, but there was a certain lift to her cheeks, almost Mongolian. I thought at once of the gorgeous Chinese-Polynesian women I had seen in Tahiti, but she did not quite fit. There was not a trace of accent in her speech when she acknowledged Anne's introduction. She was quiet and reserved and showed none of the nervousness to be expected from a youngster who faces an ordeal.

After a moment of conversation I rang for my nurse, who took the girl to a dressing room.

"I know very little about her," Anne said. "Her name is Ruth

146

Gillespie. My sister knows nothing more except that at the orphanage they said she was one of the nicest girls they had ever had. She is lovely with the children, but with us there is a kind of wall around her. I've tried to get her to talk about herself. She doesn't seem to want to."

In a few minutes the nurse opened the door to say that she was ready. Anne went with me to the examining room. "Ruthie," she said, "you don't mind if you stay here with the doctor and the nurse without me for a few minutes, do you? I really ought to run home and help my sister pack." Turning to me, she said, "Please just phone when she is ready, and I'll hurry back."

I examined the girl carefully. Everything was normal except that her heart was racing in curious contrast to her stoic exterior. Under the circumstances, I accepted that as normal, too. She did not look at me, but her glowing eyes followed my nurse's every move.

When we were finished I decided to take her back to Anne's house, almost on the way to my home, instead of interrupting Anne to come for her. Ready to leave, I spoke sharply to my little dog sleeping in the corner, a valuable schnauzer. I had taught her to come only when called in a language I had learned in Alaska years before.

"*Chako*, Mitzi," I said. "*Nesika klatawa.*" (Come, we are going.)

The dog leaped to her feet but was no quicker than the girl, who turned to face me, her eyes wide with sudden excitement.

"Oh, oh! What did you say?" she exclaimed. "*Nika kumtux mika!*" (I understand you.) She rushed up to me, her shyness gone, holding out both trembling hands, a different creature.

"Where?" she said. "Where did you learn those words? Those were my baby words ... my mother taught me ... that was our secret baby talk ... she called me *tenas*, little one ... just for us two, she said ... and now you say words to your dog that my mother said to me ... and she died when I was so little ... and I've never heard one single word like it since ... "

147

The girl was shaking, so pitifully agitated that obviously my words had touched something far deeper than mere surprise. This was extraordinary for me, too.

"'Baby talk!' I exclaimed. "Don't you know what kind of talk that is and where it comes from?"

"Oh, do you know where it comes from? That's what I want to know more than anything else in this world, because then I'll know where I've come from, too. Tell me! Tell me!"

Suddenly the girl swayed and her face was white except for the olive tinge that had puzzled me. I knew then where that had come from, too. I put my arm around her and told her to lie flat on the couch for a moment.

"*Mika kumtux?*" (You understand?) I asked as she sat up again.

"Oh yes," she cried. "Of course I understand. But how do you know these words?"

She covered her face with her hands, still trembling with excitement. I telephoned Anne. "Your Ruthie is fine," I said. "I'll drop her at your house in a few minutes. But on your way home from the train station I'd like to have you leave her at our house for the night. She needn't bring anything with her. Our foster daughter, Marie, is just about the same age. She wants to study nursing, too, and knows all the ropes. They will like each other . . . and Anne, there's another reason, too, a very important one; but please don't ask her any special questions. I'll tell you about it later."

Shortly after dinner, Ruthie arrived. Outwardly she was quiet and calm, but I could sense the excitement that for a moment she had shown in the afternoon. We told Marie to take her upstairs to rest a little while, to find pajamas, slippers and a dressing gown for her and then for both of them to come down again.

When they appeared, my wife had blackberry tea waiting and there was a fire in the grate. Apparently comforted and made to feel at home by the presence of the other girl, Ruthie opened her eyes wide with delight as she entered.

"How wonderful!" she cried. "May I . . . may I sit by the fire?" She dropped gracefully to an easy, natural position on the floor that I had seen 10 thousand times on the Indian mats in the North, her eyes begging me to explain the mystery. I was in almost as bad a state.

"I haven't heard a word of Chinook for years, either," I began. "They don't speak it this far south . . ."

"But where? Where?" she interrupted.

"Just one area in the world," I told her, "from the Columbia River north to the Southeastern Alaska coast. It's an easy useful jargon of Indian languages with French, Spanish and English words, a kind of Esperanto, going way back before the explorers of the 17th century and enlarged by the early Hudson Bay Company traders. Practically all the Natives in Southeast Alaska speak it, and many white men, too. The tribal languages are so different that Chinook is the only way they can understand each other. Now tell us how you learned it before I get faint, too."

"I learned it from my mother," she said slowly. "I thought it was just a game. It was fun to have such a big secret with her. She told me never to let the other children hear any of the words. I didn't know why. She loved to have me use them with her, though."

"Did your father know the words?"

"I don't know. I never saw my father. My mother never spoke of him," she answered quietly. "There must have been something very sad or very secret, because Mother never wanted anyone to know her. Once in a while she went to church, never anywhere else. We lived in a little house in the yard of the people she worked for. She was called Ruth, and I was Ruthie. They were the only names I knew. It's dreadful but . . . I don't . . . I don't know who I am . . . I don't even know my name. When I got older I learned about birth certificates and wanted to find mine, but I didn't know where to start because I never knew where I was born or what name to look for."

"But . . . Gillespie?" I asked, remembering the name Anne had told me.

"They gave me that name at the orphanage where I was sent when Mother died. I was just another little girl and no one knew us. They were very good to me but I missed my mother terribly. I remember her as beautiful but maybe that was just because I loved her so. She was darker than I am, and as I remember her, quite different some way.

"She used to tell me wonderful stories of the forest and the sea and of curious totems and totem poles. As I got older I realized that that suggested Indians, of course, but I read in the *Brittanica* that totems were found all over the world among 'primitive peoples.' I made up my mind that if I came from 'primitive peoples' I was going to find them. I even tried some of my words on Indians who came along in circuses, but no one ever understood. I wanted to study to be a teacher, or a nurse. I thought maybe sometime ... well ... it might sound silly, but I thought that when I found my people I could help them."

She finished her tea and gazed thoughtfully into her empty cup.

"I'm just a normal everyday girl, I think," she added, "except for this one wish that never goes away—to find out who my mother was and where she came from. I've wondered why I am so much lighter color than she was, but of course I can guess about that—he was probably white—and I think the secret of my mother's sadness must have something to do with my father. I don't like him if he made my mother suffer so. Oh, Doctor, I never talked like this before. What have you done to me?"

"I want to help you, my dear," I answered. "Are there any other clues at all?"

"Just one," she replied, "and that's the most distressing of all because I can't quite remember. Always, always when she told me stories there was a place that began with K. She said it over and over and almost always she cried when she said it and then I cried, too, but I didn't know why. I just can't remember that word. It has

150

haunted me. Maybe if I knew, I could go there and find ... "

"A place that began with K?" I said. "Ketchikan? Klawock? Klinquan?"

"No, no!" she exclaimed, "a longer name, I think. I've tried so hard ... at night when I couldn't sleep ... I've looked at every page in the atlas ... "

"*Kopet ikt?*" I ventured, though I scarcely knew why.

"Kopet-ikt!" she cried. She jumped to her feet. "Kopet-ikt! Oh, I believe that's it. That's the word that made my mother cry. Where is Kopet-ikt? Oh, please!"

I hated to tell her.

"I'm sorry, my dear," I said as gently as I could. "*Kopet ikt* is not the name of a place. It is simply Chinook for 'lonely' or 'the only one' ... and how lonely your mother must have felt, so far from her native land. I can understand her tears." Ruthie looked at me a moment and then dropped again to her place on the floor and covered her face with her hands, bending forward as if by instinct in the crouching position taken by the women of the North when they mourn. She looked so little and alone—*kopet ikt*, I thought to myself. No one spoke, and then after a few moments, "May I?" she said, looking over at the sleeping dog. "*Chako*, Mitzi, *chako!*" The little dog went to her at once and rested its head on the girl's knee, their brown eyes fixed on each other. She seemed to need something close to her, something she could touch. She said soft little words to Mitzi, who snuggled close to her. It would have been a pretty picture except for the heartsickness and bitter disappointment in the girl's face.

And then—I wondered how I could have been so dull—there flashed for the first time across my mind a possible but an almost unbelievable answer to the mystery.

"Anne Skarstad said that you are 15 and that you lived at the orphanage near her sister's home. That's in Ohio. But where did you live with your mother?"

She caught the excitement in my voice. "Oh, in Ohio," she said.

151

"Always in Ohio. Why?" She looked at me as if afraid to unleash hope again.

"Ruthie," I said, "I don't quite know. This is the strangest thing I ever heard of, too strange to be true. Don't count on it too much, not yet anyway. When I left Alaska 35 years ago to study medicine I brought out four little Indian girls, taking them to a mission school in Ohio. I tried to keep track of them but could hear about only three. The fourth one disappeared. They thought she married a white man but no one knew. No one could find her. She was the one of the four I was most interested in. If that one was your mother I know where she lived as a child. Does Kasaan mean anything to you?"

"Kasaan?" she said intently. "Were there totem poles there? Lots of totem poles? It seems to me ... "

"Many of them," I told her and immediately another picture, an extraordinary one, flashed before me, swept me back nearly 40 years to a wild night off the coast of Prince of Wales Island when a sudden southeaster lashed the strait. The little boat that was carrying four of us north for assessment work was swamped, and after six hours of clinging to the side of the boat in that icy water in March, battered by driftwood, we were thrown exhausted on the beach miles from any settlement. The next day a party of Indians from the village of Kasaan happened by in their boat and carried us to safety.

When we went ashore at Kasaan to rest a few days, the brightest and most attractive Native child I had ever seen was in and out of my cabin constantly, bringing me food and water or sometimes just a smile. We all called her *tenas*, little one, exactly as the girl sitting before me had in turn been called. A year or two later it was partly at my suggestion that she was selected as one of the four to "go Outside" for an education. I did not remember the child's real name but I was sure that I could find a way to get it.

Now I told Ruthie the whole story, with all the details I could summon, hoping that they would revive some corresponding bits.

152

As I did there came gradually to her mind dim little childhood memories of tales that her mother had told her—of streams so crowded with salmon that the black bears flipped them out with their paws, of rain and wind and of waves higher than a house. She sat almost breathless before me, fascinated, trembling with eagerness. We talked for hours, and every little fragment in her memory fitted into the picture. I gradually became convinced that the factors of age, of speech, of Ohio and of that one girl's disappearance could hardly mean anything else. There was very little question of her identity when I finally insisted that she go to bed.

All this happened five years ago. Yesterday a letter came.
Dear Doctor:
I have arrived in Kasaan. There is an elderly Native man here who actually remembers picking up four half-drowned prospectors along the coast many years ago, exactly as you described it. He can't be certain which was the *tenas* who helped care for you. But I have been to the mission in Ketchikan and I am quite sure that I have found what is left of my mother's family. I know that I have found myself. There is a little school here and I am to be the teacher. After all this time I have found the place where I am really needed.

My love, my warm and appreciative love, for you and your family—and a loving pat for that beautiful Mitzi who, sleeping in the corner, was the first link in the extraordinary chain that has brought this happiness to me.

Ruthie

Acknowledgements

In addition to his years as "miner, preacher, doctor, teacher," Frederic Loomis was a highly regarded author, and his Alaska tales should gain him a new following. The stories are his own, told with an engaging combination of boyish enthusiasm and reflective wisdom, but these 50 or 60 years after they were drafted it seemed prudent to double-check their historical context. The books listed here were useful in that process, and research was eased throughout by the generous cooperation of a number of helpful people.

Many thanks to The Rev. Gary S. Herbst, rector, and Martha Clark at St. John's Episcopal church, Ketchikan; Virginia MacDonald and Mary Parsons, Episcopal Diocese of Alaska, Fairbanks; Jennifer Peters, assistant archivist for references and public service, Archives of the Episcopal Church, Austin, Texas; Toni Kessler, University of Michigan Transcript and Certification Office, Ann Arbor; and Edward Copenhagen of Boston College.

Heartfelt gratitude as well to the staffs of the public libraries in Berkeley, Grass Valley, Pleasant Hill, San Francisco and Walnut Creek, Calif., and Bandon, Ore.; to the crew at the J. Porter Shaw Library of the San Francisco Maritime National Historical Park; to Bill Sturm of the Oakland History Room, Oakland (Calif.) Public Library; to Anna Poe of the Alaska Native Language Center, University of Alaska Fairbanks; to Ann Shelton, head of Historical Collections, Alaska State Library, Juneau; and—definitely not least—to David Kiffer, executive director of Historic Ketchikan Inc., Ketchikan, Alaska, whose maternal great-grandparents mined at Dolomi and Niblack on Prince of Wales Island and who as a writer and editor himself understood our obsession with getting it right.

References

Alaska A to Z, from the editors of *The Milepost*; researched and written by Angela M. Herb, Vernon Publications Inc., Bellevue, Wash., 1993

Alaska Atlas & Gazeteer, DeLorme, Yarmouth, Maine, 1998

The Alaskan Churchman, Episcopal Diocese of Alaska, Fairbanks, Vols. 9 (Feb./May 1915, p. 83), 10 (Nov. 1915, pp. 16-17) and 11 (Aug. 1917, pp. 111-116)

Alaska's Native People, The Alaska Geographic Society, Volume 6, Number 3, Anchorage, 1979

A Century of Faith, 1895-1995 / Centennial Commemorative, Episcopal Diocese of Alaska, Centennial Press, Fairbanks, 1995

Chinook: A History and Dictionary of the Northwest Coast Trade Jargon, by Edward Harper Thomas, Binford & Mort, Publishers, Portland, Ore., 1935, 1954, 1970

The Chinook jargon and how to use it: A complete and exhaustive lexicon of the oldest trade language of the American continent, by George Coombs Shaw, Rainier Printing Company Inc., Seattle, 1909

Confessions of an Alaska Bootlegger, by Ralph Soberg, Hardscratch Press, Walnut Creek, Calif., 1990

Dictionary of Alaskan English, by Russell Tabbert, The Denali Press, Juneau 1991

Field Guide to Alaskan Wildflowers, by Verna E. Pratt, Alaskakrafts Publishing, Anchorage, 1989

Geology and Mineral Deposits of the Dolomi Area, Prince of Wales Island, Alaska, by Gordon Herreid, Division of Mine and Minerals, Dept. of Natural Resources, State of Alaska, June 1967

Ghost Towns of Alaska, by Mary G. Balcom, Adams Press, Chicago, 1965

Gilbert Said / An oldtimer's tales of the Haida-Tlingit waterways of Alaska, by Marian L. Swain, Hardscratch Press, Walnut Creek, Calif., 1992

Indians of the Northwest Coast, by Philip Drucker, published for The American Museum of Natural History, 1955, McGraw-Hill Book Co., Inc., New York, Toronto, London

Indians of the Northwest Coast (originally published in Germany as *Indianer der Nordwestküste*), text by Peter R. Gerber (translated by Barbara Fritzmeier), photographs by Maximilien Burggman, Facts on File Publications, New York, 1989

The Ketchikan and Wrangell Mining Districts, Alaska, by F.E. and C.W. Wright, U.S. Geological Survey Bulletin 347 (p. 210), 1908

The Man of Alaska / Peter Trimble Rowe, by The Right Rev. Thomas Jenkins, D.D., retired bishop of Nevada, Morehouse-Gorham Co., New York, 1943

The Peraltan, published by Peralta Hospital Association, Oakland, Calif., Volume XIII, No. 2, Nov. 1972

Preliminary Report of the Ketchikan Mining District, Alaska, by Alfred H. Brooks, U.S. Geological Survey, Washington, 1902

Report on the Progress of Investigations of Mineral Resources in Alaska in 1905, by Alfred H. Brooks, U.S.G.S., Washington, 1906

South/Southeast Alaska, The Alaska Geographic Society, Volume 14, Number 2, Anchorage, 1987

The White Pass: Gateway to the Klondike, by Roy Minter, University of Alaska Press, 1987

Also by Frederic Loomis (out of print at present):

Consultation Room, Alfred A. Knopf, New York, 1939

The Bond Between Us / The Third Component, Alfred A. Knopf, New York, 1942

In a Chinese Garden, Loomis Book Co., Piedmont, Calif., 1946

The Best Medicine, Loomis Book Co. (compiled by Evalyn Loomis in 1949; includes an earlier version of a chapter in this book titled "We Can Do It!" which appeared first in *Reader's Digest*, Nov. 1947)

Among Dr. Loomis' papers were a number of letters of appreciation from his readers that provide an intriguing glimpse into the era as well as into their own lives. A sampling:

Dear Dr Loomis:

Recently my wife brought home a book called "Consultation Room" and recommended it to me. As I thought it was just another of those doctor's autobiographies I did not open it until I was without other resource. Pretty soon I began enjoying it so much that I read it through almost without intermission.

I then became curious as to the author and when I saw the name a little bug of memory began to stir in my brain. Dr. Loomis—he was on the staff of the Alameda County Hospital. He was the man who insisted that we treat the maternity patients there—all paupers—just as tho they were private patients paying fees; a lesson that I have passed on to many internes.

You have no reason to remember me. I was interne and then resident in 1922 and 1923. Dr Richards may remember me as the interne who stubbornly adhered to a (correct) diagnosis of ectopic pregnancy in the face of much opposition. Ever after he would introduce me in the following fashion: "This is Dr Labensky. Dr Labensky is a Yale man. You can always tell a Yale man—but you can't tell him much."

The two years I spent at the County were a source of much pleasure and benefit and still remain a happy remembrance. My very best wishes to all of the staff whom I knew, even to Mr Jensen.

I would appreciate it greatly if you would autograph the attached book and return it to me.

Sincerely,
Alfred Labensky, M.D., New London, Conn. (telephone 7894)

July 29, 1944

Dear Dr. Loomis:

It is only after considerable debate with myself that I attempt to contact you to make the request that you permit me to forward to you a recently attained volume of "Consultation Room" that you may inscribe on its flyleaf your personal autograph. I wish to present this volume to my daughter on her 29th birthday—the anniversary of the day you delivered her 6½ squalling pounds in Ann Arbor, Michigan.

I do not presume that you remember the occasion—a tiny dot that goes to make up the huge mass of your similar experiences, but an epochal event in my memory as well as that of her mother, Bessie. You may remember me, however, as a purveyor of groceries that partly supplied your table from the Huron Street Grocery; yeh! the fellow who stretched his shoestring too far by opening a second store near the Campus and was caught a couple of years later by the local depression resulting from the Army's draft of the major portion of the Student Body—and had to accept business defeat!

This little daughter who responded that morning to your encouraging spank with such an enthusiastic wail that I (whom you had detailed to the ether cone because the practical nurse we had to resort to due to the terrible flu epidemic ravaging through the nurses ranks of the University Hospital, insulted your professional pride by her clumsiness) informed her half conscious mother that we had another son—which error you quickly corrected much to my chagrin—is now the proud mother of 3 Campbell sons, 6, 7 and 8 prox. years old. She will treasure this volume which will surely have an heirloom destiny in her family.

Bessie and I closed our marital record when the children reached near maturity, and she has been for many years the happy and contented wife of my very dear friend, Victor Appel. She is also informed and happily approves this request to which I most deeply hope you will comply. In fact, it was she who discovered the edition and, after she and her husband had read it, loaned it to me: MAN, IT'S WONDERFUL!

Very sincerely yours,

Russell J. Smith, St. Louis, 4, Missouri

(In a subsequent letter Russell Smith invited Frederic Loomis to fly with him sometime in his Luscomb airplane: "I took my solo flight on my fiftieth birthday, so I get a bigger kick out of it than the average youngster, because they will never know what it is to make sales calls with a horse and buggy.")

My dear Dr. Loomis: Oct. 19, 1943

You wouldn't remember me as I was only one of the many student nurses at Ann Arbor while you were in school. But I cannot forget you. Why? Here is why. You never were too busy to be kind and polite even when a student nurse asked you questions the answers to which she should have known. If you didn't have time at the moment to answer the question, I remember you used to keep a notebook and pencil with you, and down went the question, the nurse's name and where she worked. Later on you always hunted up the nurse and answered her questions. How could I forget when I was one of the student nurses who used to ask you questions.

Then too, I remember working on Women's Surgical floor a good deal of the time and if you found you were going to be late at lunch time, how you never failed to phone your home to let your wife know.

One doesn't forget thoughtfulness like that. So, when I saw a book in Rock Springs, Wyo., where I was working a few years ago, with your name as the author I bought it at once. Since then, both doctors and nurses have read and enjoyed it immensely. Both it and "The Bond Between Us" are still going the rounds and the end is not yet. Thanks so much for writing them. They are as good as any tonic. Dr. Lauzer, Rock Springs, and Dr. Stewart, Saginaw, Mich., are two who have enjoyed knowing you and reading your books. Also Mrs. MacNamara, R.N., of Saginaw.

Thanks again for writing those books.

Sincerely yours,
Vera Schell, R.N., Saginaw, Mich.

Sept. 14, 1944

Dear Sir,

Your book, "The Bond Between Us / The Third Component," is a very good book. You may be quite surprised to learn that a great many of the so-called G.I.'s are reading your books. You've explained to us things that a lot of us didn't know much about or else had mixed up. Thank you for putting your experiences down on paper and thus serving mankind again. Right now there is a waiting list at our post library. We all are required to finish it in three days but that's unnecessary, for we usually finish it in one.

Another G.I. with his eyes opened,

Pfc. Samuel R. McHenry, 13111491
Squadron E, Ephrata Army Air Base, Ephrata, Wash.

MINER, PREACHER, DOCTOR, TEACHER

Project coordinator and editor: Jackie Pels
Book design and production: David R. Johnson
Mapmaker: John W. Boring

Loomis family photos, except the c. 1913 views of Oakland,
Calif., in Chapter XVI, which are courtesy of the Oakland
History Room of the Oakland Public Library.

"Through a Glacier Window," Chapter X, is by Harrie C. Barley,
company photographer for the White Pass and Yukon Railway
between 1898 and 1900. In *The White Pass: Gateway to the
Klondike* (University of Alaska Press, 1987), author Roy Minter
says, "One of the first accidents at Rocky Point was suffered by
Barley, the company's photographer, who had already gained a
reputation for bringing work to a full stop wherever he appeared.
His huge box camera, tripod, and heavy case of glass negatives
were a familiar sight along the grade ..." A Loomis family album
contains several of Barley's prints.

The two blue-toned snapshots on the cover are cyanotypes,
developed by a process popular at the turn of the 19th century.
The beach scene with totems was taken on Frederic and Edith
Loomis' honeymoon trip to the Haida village of Kasaan,
Prince of Wales Island.

Composition by Archetype Typography, Berkeley, California
Printed by Inkworks Press, Berkeley, California
Alkaline pH recycled paper (Strathmore Elements)

Hardscratch Press
2358 Banbury Place
Walnut Creek, CA 94598
phone/fax 925/935-3422